CW01332870

CHRONICLE
OF THE
ISLAY GOLF CLUB
AND THE
MACHRIE LINKS

BY
JOHN CUBBAGE

Copyright © John Cubbage 1996
All rights reserved.
ISBN 0 9528719 0 4

Published by Islay Golf Club, Isle of Islay

Printed by S.K.I. Graphics (Scotland) Ltd.
Glasgow G40, Scotland

Acknowledgements

Firstly I wish to thank Harry Cockburn for salvaging the Minute Book, without which the early history of the Islay Golf Club would have been incomplete. I am also grateful to the late Freda Ramsay for providing excerpts from the Kildalton Estate papers, to David Boyd, factor to Islay Estate, for access to early estate records, to the Museum of Islay Life for valuable information from their early golf magazines and to the Mitchell Library, Glasgow, for access to their records.

The excerpts from newspapers and magazines have considerably enhanced the basic data from the Minutes. I would also like to record my appreciation of Brian Morrison's help in providing information on the early days of Stanley P. Morrison and for allowing access to the Morrison Bowmore files relative to Machrie.

I thank Murdo MacPherson for the initial invitation to get involved and for access to his records and photographs. United Distillers are thanked for providing the photograph of Sir P. J. Mackie and a special thanks goes to Mr. Gordon McIntosh of Keepers of The Quaich for his important contribution to the story of the Lagavulin Quaich and for supplying a photograph of it.

The Chronicles would have been incomplete without the valuable contributions from both past and present members of Islay G.C. Their verbal and written contributions and the loan of photographs and brochures brought the whole story to life. I therefore sincerely thank: John Calder, John Campbell, Mr. and Mrs. W. F. Fry of Dorset, Scott Grier, T. Melville Lang, D. McArthur, Mrs. A. MacCalman, John MacFarlane, Roy and Robin MacGregor, John MacIntyre Snr. and Jnr., Sam McKinlay, Alec Mackinnon, Brian and Tim Morrison and Gilbert Stevenson. I would also like to thank the contributors to Chapter 11 for their special recollections and memories. My apologies to anyone whose name has inadvertently been omitted. Photographers Eric Thorburn and Fraser McArthur are thanked for permission to use their excellent photographs.

I acknowledge the contribution of previous Hon. Secretaries for their diligent recording of the Minutes, some more detailed than others. The essential link between the writer and Islay was provided by Tom Dunn the current Hon. Secretary of the Golf Club. The Club are fortunate to have such a dedicated enthusiast at the helm. Many thanks Tom.

I must thank my wife Olive for her patience (tested to the full!), her advice and constructive criticism, also my daughter Sheila for her computing skills and help in editing. She pulled the complete Chronicles together onto disc, ready for printing.

My final thanks go to the successive Committees who have continued over recent years to express their determination to see the Chronicles published.

J.C.

The Captain's Foreword

In 1991 the Islay Golf Club celebrated its Centenary and to commemorate the event the Committee decided to produce the 'Chronicles of the Islay Golf Club and the Machrie Links' covering the previous 100 years.

I have been a member of the Islay Golf Club since 1956 and Machrie has given my whole family wonderful memories of golf, friendship and conviviality. It now gives me great pleasure to read that this spirit of goodwill has prevailed since 1891.

The Committee are indebted especially to John Cubbage, Golf Historian, for his diligent research over several years, to his daughter, Dr. Sheila Hamilton, for her skills on the computer, to all contributors to the Chronicles, to Tom Dunn, Hon. Secretary of Islay G.C. for his drive and enthusiasm and finally to Mr. M. King of the Machrie Hotel and Golf Course for his support.

I hope that everyone who reads these Chronicles will continue to support the Machrie Links thus ensuring a sequel in 2091.

Ralph Middleton
Captain, Islay Golf Club. 1995-96

Ralph Middleton
(by Fraser McArthur)

Introduction

In many Golf Club histories there is often a distinct lack of information about the earlier years of the Club, often due to the loss of the Minutes. This situation was avoided on Islay, thanks to Harry Cockburn of Morrison Bowmore Distillers who retrieved the original Minutes of the Islay Golf Club from a box of unwanted material which was about to be discarded at the Head Office in Glasgow. This, along with the quite abnormal number of references to Islay golf revealed by research, ensured that the first thirty years of the colourful history of Islay golf and its characters were well documented.

When the Minute book [1891 to 1929] was passed to me because of my interest in the history of golf, I immediately realised its importance. A chance meeting with Murdo MacPherson at the airport on Islay set the history in motion with the intention of publishing after the Centenary year. However, indecision, lack of finance and committment delayed the completion of the history until the Islay G.C., decided to proceed on their own, even although the Centenary was past.

I have tried to make the Chronicles of interest to a wider audience by broadening the scope to include relevant details of the companies and individuals whose influence on the Golf Club was significant. The details of the Machrie Hotel and its owners have been included since history has shown how their success is dependent on a successful Golf Club and vice versa.

Inevitably there may be some inaccuracies in spite of every attempt having been made to check the facts and the identification of individuals in the photographs. My apologies go to anyone whose name or golfing success has been omitted, including the ladies about whom little information was forthcoming other than the rare and brief mention in the Minutes.

Finally, I hope that all readers will get as much enjoyment from the Chronicles as I did in researching and writing them. To those golfers unfamiliar with the magic of golf on the Machrie Links, I suggest that their golfing life will be incomplete without a visit to Islay. I trust that present and past members of the Islay G.C. will ensure that succeeding generations are encouraged to maintain the tradition of family golf on Islay as depicted in the Chronicles.

J.C.

Contents

	Page
Acknowledgements	iii
Captain's Foreword	iv
Introduction	v
Chapter One, Gowf comes to Islay	1
Chapter Two, 19th Century Gowf – The Last Decade	14
Chapter Three, Dawn of a New Century	39
Chapter Four, The Great War Period	62
Chapter Five, Between the Wars	66
Chapter Six, War and Peace	82
Chapter Seven, A Run-up to the Centenary	95
Chapter Eight, The Kildalton Challenge Cross	114
Chapter Nine, Sir Peter Jeffrey Mackie and the Mackie Quaich	133
Chapter Ten, The Machrie Links	137
Chapter Eleven, Memories	151
Chapter Twelve, Centenary Celebration	165
Postscript	175
Appendices	176

Islay Golf Club.

CHAPTER ONE

GOWF COMES TO ISLAY

Forming a Golf Club
Golf had been played in Scotland since the 15th century principally along the East coast links land but it was 1744 before Scotland's first golf club, The Company of Edinburgh Golfers, was formed. In the West, although the Glasgow Golf Club had been formed in 1787, playing on Glasgow Green, the first club on the coast did not appear until 1851 at Prestwick. About this time the cheap gutta percha ball replaced the expensive feather ball. The laying of new coastal railway lines provided quick and cheap transport to the new golf courses. As a result the popularity of the game increased and a trickle of new clubs became a torrent in the 1890s throughout the country. It was inevitable that this golf boom should spread to Islay and to all the other popular holiday islands in the West all about the same time.

When Old Tom Morris was asked for his advice on how to form a golf club his reply was always the same: "The best way to form a club is to get as many of your friends together as possible then advertise such a club has been instituted." He could have added some other necessities such as a generous wealthy benefactor with plenty of links land adjacent to the sea and an interest in the prosperity of the local community, an organiser to get things moving and last but not least several dedicated local enthusiasts to establish and maintain the initial impetus and to steer the golf club through its early years. All of these essential ingredients were present on Islay.

The prime mover and organiser in the formation of Islay Golf Club was Peter Jeffrey Mackie of Lagavulin Distillery and Mackie & Co. in association with John Ramsay of Kildalton, a wealthy benefactor and landowner on the island. According to the late Freda Ramsay, John Ramsay's grand-daughter-in-law, it was James Higginbotham, a keen golfer from Prestwick and a regular visitor to Kildalton, who first suggested to John Ramsay that he should consider forming a

John Ramsay of Kildalton

John Ramsay of Kildalton

golf course and club at Machrie. However, the key figure was undoubtedly Peter Mackie. Both Mackie and John Ramsay had been associates in the whisky industry and politics for some time and shared strong interests in the well-being of the local community. It is likely that informal discussion had been taking place for some time before Mackie and Ramsay started seriously to formulate ideas for the Golf Club.

The first entry in the Minute Book in Mackie's handwriting records the agreement on the lease of the land.

'At a meeting between John Ramsay Esq. of Kildalton and Peter Jeffrey Mackie at Lagavulin in September 1890 it was agreed that the said John Ramsay would grant to Peter Jeffrey Mackie on behalf of a golf club to be formed on Islay a lease of Machir links for five years from 15th May 1891 at the annual rental of one pound per annum (9th December 1890).'

The first intimation to the local public of the impending arrival of golf on Islay came in an article in the *Campbeltown Courier* of 8th November 1890:

'A well known Glasgow gentleman, an enthusiastic golfer is at present actively interesting himself in the formation of a golfing club to play on the Machry links near Port Ellen.....we understand a prominent Edinburgh golfer who has visited it is said to consider it will make one of the finest links in the West of Scotland.'

The previous week that 'Glasgow gentleman' alias Peter Jeffrey Mackie had visited the island and obtained upwards of £100 in subscription towards the formation of the club. A further article in the same paper on 29th November 1890 stated that golfer Willie Campbell, who was the professional and greenkeeper at Ranfurly Castle Golf Club, Bridge of Weir, had visited Islay the previous week to view the ground etc. and his report had been most favourable, suggesting that the Machrie Links with its natural links features had great potential. Indeed legend has it that when Willie Campbell first stood on top of one of the sand dunes and surveyed the luscious green valleys between countless sand dunes running for miles alongside the golden sands of Laggan Bay his first words were: "This place was made for Gowf." His report to Mr. Mackie was brief but worth reporting in full:

'I visited Islay as you ordered me and have much to report it is the best ground for a golf course that I have ever had the pleasure of viewing. Sir, I can say that you could make for very little money one of the best courses in Scotland as it will need very little more than cutting the `puttin` greens and making a bridge hear and there. If this was dunn you could play golf the next day.

    Your servant,
    Signed, Willie Campbell.'

This visit and report earned Willie the princely sum of £3 12s. including expenses but no points for his spelling.

Armed with Campbell's report plus promises of subscriptions P. J. Mackie held a meeting on 21st January 1891 with Peter Reid, Factor to Kildalton Estate, Mr. Lachlan McCuaig, proprietor of the White Hart Hotel, Port Ellen and Mr. D. McLeod, proprietor of Islay Hotel, Port Ellen. It was agreed that Mr. Mackie form a club and take the matter in hand, the club to be called the Islay Golf Club. Mr. Mackie was given full powers to act till such time as a Committee be appointed and the club take possession of the Green. Peter Reid agreed to become Secretary with Mr. McCuaig being Treasurer 'at the request' of Peter J. Mackie. Thus, the decision was made by these four to proceed with the formation of the Islay Golf Club.

All the added necessities were now in place, the organiser, the local enthusiasts, suitable links and the wealthy benefactor, John Ramsay. Mr. Mackie's next job was to follow Old Tom's advice, contact his wealthy influential friends, get their agreement to join the club and then advertise for members. First of all, he needed a figurehead as President and who better to invite than the Duke of Argyll. His Grace replied on 22nd January 1891:

'Sit if the use of my name is of any service to you in connection with the Golf Club of Islay you are welcome to it. But I do not subscribe to such local purposes.
Signed 'Argyll'.'

Mr. Mackie must have been disappointed at this refusal to contribute financially to get the Islay Golf Club off the ground. However, he set about forming the committee of prominent names of friends and business associates who were willing to have their names put forward. This 'advertised' committee was as follows:

Hon. President
His Grace the Duke of Argyll K.G.K.T.
Vice-Presidents
J. Wingfield Malcolm Esq. M.P.
John Ramsay. Esq., of Kildalton
Committee
Major Ayshford Wise, Islay House, Captain
R. L. Watson, Dundee
J. R. Findlay of Aberdour
W. A. Robertson, 45 West Nile Street, Glasgow
Cyril Wintle, Thatched House Club, St. James Street, SW
W. Morrison, 77 St. Vincent Street, Glasgow
W. Sanderson, Leith
P. J. Mackie, Lagavulin, Islay
Secretary
Peter Reid, Factor, Port Ellen
Treasurer
Lachlan McCuaig, Port Ellen, Islay

These 'original Office-Bearers' appear only to have been figureheads as there is no record of them attending any meeting.

The expected cash inflow did not arrive from the above names except for those with a local interest. In total £170 was subscribed, equivalent to some £7000 in present day terms and was made up as follows: -

D. McLeod	£50
L. McCuaig	£50
P. J. Mackie	£25
Chas. Morrison of Islay	£10
Major Wise, Islay House	£10
John Ramsay of Kildalton	£10
Alec Hay of Ardbeg	£5
David MacBrayne	£5
W. A. Robertson	£5

Those who donated £10 or more became Original Life Members of the Club.

The list of subscribers was fully representative of the Islay economy. Messrs. McLeod and McCuaig had most to gain from the venture as they were the proprietors of the two principal hotels in Port Ellen, just 3 1/2 miles from the site chosen for the golf course. The wealthy landowners, Charles Morrison and John Ramsay, owned adjoining estates of Islay and Kildalton and Oa which together covered some two-thirds of the island. As the principal industry of the island was the production of malt whisky it was important and natural that it should be represented. Messrs Mackie and Hay were proprietors of Lagavulin and Ardbeg Distilleries. There were eight distilleries on Islay, making it one of the most concentrated areas of whisky production in Scotland. The unique and distinct peat flavoured Islay Malts have established a niche in Scotch Whisky as one of the three designated types of Scotch. The others are Lowland Malt and Highland Malt. It was recognised that visitors from the mainland would be essential for the success of the Golf Club and hence the reason for the presence of David MacBrayne who was owner of David MacBrayne & Co., the principal shipping company serving the island.

An early decision was made to appoint a golf professional/ keeper of the green. Adverts in *Golf* for a professional for the summer months of the first year produced four applications from Bob Ferguson of Musselburgh, A.C. Brown, R. Laik and J. Martin of Musselburgh. Of these Bob Ferguson was the most famous golfer having won the Open three times in 1880, 1881 and 1882 and lost a play-off to Willie Fernie in 1883. Possibly for financial reasons he didn't get the job and J. Martin was picked 'in deference to the findings of the sub-committee'. His terms were not exactly generous being 22/- per week starting 15th May 1891, £1 allowance for travelling to and from Islay, one month's notice either side before dismissal and Martin to be allowed to charge at such rates for teaching as the committee fix!! He was also to 'make himself useful and keep the greens'.

Golf had not yet reached the stage of separating the professional's job from that of 'Keeper of the Green'. The professionals of this era generally came from the caddie ranks, and many in fact still caddied as well. The better ones were in demand for money challenge matches with and without amateurs. The stakes of up to £100 were substantial for those days and there was much on course betting on the results. Those few open stroke competitions which were held, other than the Open, were run by private golf clubs. Prize money was low and unlike today the prizes did not extend far down the field. Isolated on an island, as Martin was, there would be few opportunities for him to augment his income in any of these ways.

By the time John Martin arrived on Islay on 15th May 1891, the Golf Club was up and running. Willie Campbell had been paid £2.6s. for another visit to the Machrie and £5 travelling expenses (compare the £1 paid to the professional for travel from Musselburgh!). A pretty basic small corrugated iron clubhouse had been purchased from P. & R. Fleming & Co. of Glasgow and erected at a cost of £68.18s. Annual Subscriptions were fixed at £1.1s. with no entry fee. Life membership was offered at £10. This prompted subscriber David MacBrayne to contribute another £5 to qualify for Life Membership.

In an attempt to get more members an extensive advertising campaign was initiated in newspapers and golf magazines. The eventual cost was £29.18s.11d., almost half the cost of the new clubhouse!

Opening of the Machrie course

The date picked for the opening of the golf course was Friday, 22nd May 1891. But before that could happen Mr. Mackie needed two prominent professionais to publicise the course and to play a challenge match over Machrie. His choice was obvious. Get the two best professional match players in the West of Scotland, make the stakes high and their participation would be guaranteed. First choice was quite naturally the course designer Willie Campbell from Bridge of Weir. Willie was considered one of the best players of his era who was rarely defeated in match play. His record in stroke play was not so good as witnessed in the 1887 Open at his home course Prestwick. Apparently sailing home the likely winner with three holes to play, he heeled a shot into a bunker, took 4 to get out and ran up an eight. He finished third, three shots behind the winner, Willie Park Jnr. of

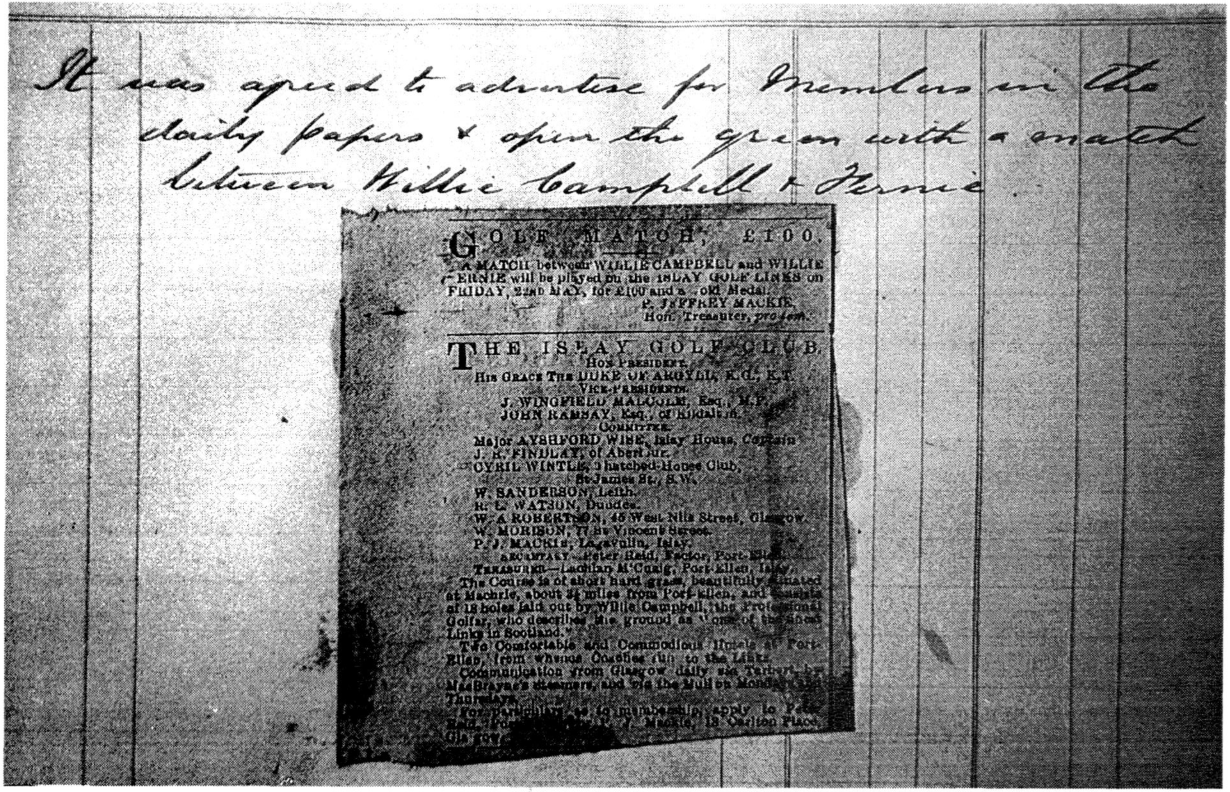

It was agreed to advertise for Members in the daily papers & open the green with a match between Willie Campbell & Fernie.

GOLF MATCH, £100.

A MATCH between WILLIE CAMPBELL and WILLIE FERNIE will be played on the ISLAY GOLF LINKS on FRIDAY, 22nd MAY, for £100 and a Gold Medal.

P. JEFFREY MACKIE,
Hon. Treasurer, pro tem.

THE ISLAY GOLF CLUB.

HON PRESIDENT.
His Grace The DUKE OF ARGYLL, K.G., K.T.
VICE-PRESIDENTS.
J. WINGFIELD MALCOLM, Esq., M.P.
JOHN RAMSAY, Esq., of Kildalton.
COMMITTEE.
Major AYSHFORD WISE, Islay House, Captain
J. R. FINDLAY, of Aberlour.
CYRIL WINTLE, Thatched-House Club, St James St., S.W.
W. SANDERSON, Leith.
R. L. WATSON, Dundee.
W. A. ROBERTSON, 45 West Nile Street, Glasgow.
W. MORISON, 77 St Vincent Street.
P. J. MACKIE, Lagavulin, Islay.
SECRETARY—Peter Reid, Factor, Port-Ellen.
TREASURER—Lachlan M'Cuaig, Port-Ellen, Islay.

The Course is of short hard grass, beautifully situated at Machrie, about 3½ miles from Port-Ellen, and consists of 18 holes laid out by Willie Campbell, the Professional Golfer, who describes the ground as "one of the finest Links in Scotland."

Two Comfortable and Commodious Hotels at Port-Ellen, from whence Coaches run to the Links.

Communication from Glasgow daily via Tarbert by MacBrayne's steamers, and via the Mull on Mondays and Thursdays.

For particulars as to membership, apply to Peter Reid, [illegible] P. J. Mackie, 18 Carlton Place, Glasgow.

Extract from Minute Book

Musselburgh. As a sequel to the 1887 Open, Horace Hutchison, a very prominent English amateur golfer of the period, later told Bernard Darwin that after this round he found Willie Campbell and his caddie sitting on pails in the professional's shop with tears streaming down their faces. It has been suggested that this was the inspiration for the original cartoon character 'Oor Wullie' of the *Sunday Post* who is often depicted crestfallen and sitting on a bucket.

Mackie's chosen opponent for Campbell was Willie Fernie (Troon) who had prevented Bob Ferguson winning his fourth successive Open in 1883. A birdie two at the last hole in a 36 hole play-off at Musselburgh gave Fernie his only Open win and he was second four times.

The stakes for the match were high - £100 to the winner plus a gold medal - so there was no problem getting the professionals to agree the challenge. It is likely that the first question thereafter from St Andrews-born Willie Fernie would be, "Islay, where is it?" and quickly followed by, "How do I get there and how long does it take?" In April 1891, an article in *The Scotsman* advertising the course, gave the answers:

> '...leave Glasgow at 8.30am by train to Gourock, embark by the SS Columba for East Tarbert, Loch Fyne which was reached given fine weather by noon. A fifteen minute drive by coach followed to West Tarbert where the SS Glencoe was waiting to take you to Port Ellen where you arrived some 4 hours later , i.e. about 4.30pm. Alternatively those for whom a round of the Mull has no terrors may prefer to travel by the Islay, leaving Glasgow in the late afternoon and reaching the island shortly after midnight.'

The build up to the opening of the course was good and the advertising extensive. The first article appeared in the *Evening Despatch* on Thursday, 23rd April 1891 entitled, 'The New Golf Course in Islay'. A sketch plan was shown giving the layout and the lengths of each hole. This sketch was prepared from an accurately marked plan provided by the Secretary Peter Reid. Unusually a further sketch was also shown giving in section the longitudinal profile of six of the holes. At 6,040 yards the course was long by late 19th century standards and strangely , contained no holes under 200 yards long. The longest hole, the 13th, was only 435 yards but uniquely, consideration was given to perhaps appeasing the tigers and big hitters of the time by providing alternative longer holes at the 8th and 9th which increased the total to an incredible 6,690 yards. This would almost certainly have made it the longest course in the country but these two optional holes do not appear to have survived for any great time. This is not surprising given the capabilities of the gutty balls and wooden shafted clubs of the day. These holes were not even used in the forthcoming Professional challenge match.

The *Evening Despatch* went on to describe the natural features of 'acres and acres of sandhills, knolls and hollows covered with short grass mixed sometimes but not very often with bent and at other places with moss'. The course was 'likened in many respects to Machrihanish with the same sporting characters, natural beauties as well as natural hazards'. The reporter was honest in his description of the negative features:

'As in all new courses, the green requires a good deal of attention before the turf will be perfect and in places the bottom of the links is rather soft and foggy ...... the rabbit holes with which the links abound may give more trouble for they are numerous - the links forming a rabbit warren on a large scale!'

At this stage the holes had not been named and surprisingly in the description of the holes no mention is made of the first hole, later known as Mount Zion, which was destined to be feared by amateur and professional. Those golfers familiar with the present course will recognise the description of the sixth hole:

'No timid golfer need hope to negotiate successfully such hazards as that, for example, which faces the player at the tee going to the sixth hole. The hill is fifty feet in height, the side facing the player is of loose sand capable of accounting for almost any number of strokes and it lies directly in the line of play. Crossed it must be and 'carried' from the tee it can, provided always the presence of danger does not unnerve the player and cause him to 'foozle'. If he does duff it he can but make the best of a bad job and vow that he will do better at the next hole.'

This hole was of course later named the Scotsman's Maiden supposedly because of its similarity with the 'Maiden' hole at Royal St George's, Sandwich, established in 1887. The writer's vague recollection of playing the Sandwich Maiden 40 years ago is of a very high grassy dune of similar height but with a longer carry from the tee. The Rev. John Kerr, writing in 1893, suggests the Islay title was given to recognise the great interest taken by *The Scotsman* newspaper through its golf correspondent W. Croal, a frequent visitor to Machrie. The likelihood is that it was a bit of both, the Maiden coming first and the Scotsman being added later.

A further article in *The Scotsman* in April 1891, entitled 'Islay and Golf', suggests the writer had possibly already experienced the delights and hazards of the Machrie Links. He notes:

'that the new Islay golf course deserves to be popular there cannot be the shadow of any doubt. It requires only to be known to be appreciated and once its acquaintance is made, there is little fear of its being suddenly or lightly dropped.'

A maxim which is possibly more true today than it ever was. The correspondent was not encouraging the poorer golfer to visit viz. :

'The regular duffer would assuredly spend so much time in freeing himself from difficulties that a full summer day would barely suffice for him to make the journey of 18 holes. But to the expert players the variety of hazards to be met with would be a source of delight and the sporting character of the green would obtain for Machrie a secure place in his good graces.'

He continues:

'They had better be clear what they go for before they set out. Port Ellen is not North Berwick and there is nothing in common between the fashionable East Coast watering place in the season and the port of Islay. But Port Ellen is a pretty little place, all the same - a trifle old world in some things no doubt, but still a very comfortable and snug retreat for anyone in search of health and golf. Excellent hotel accommodation it has. The White Hart for example is one of the most comfortable houses one could sleep in; and the landlord Mr. McCuaig, who is by general consent looked upon as the Admiral of the Port is a veritable mine of information on subjects touching the history and the welfare of the island.'

So the net was cast for prospective visitors and golfers and the stage set for the grand opening.

Shortly before noon Mrs. Lucy Ramsay formally opened the links by driving the first ball using a club with a silver head which was presented to her by the club as a memento of the formal opening. (The club unfortunately is not in the late Mrs. Freda Ramsay's possession; she thought it had been passed on to other members of the family some time ago). Those present included Mr. Ramsay of Kildalton, Mrs. and Miss Ramsay, Captain Graham of Lagavulin, Major Wise, Captain of the Islay Golf Club, Mr. P.J. Mackie, Councillor McCuaig and Peter Reid. The important dignitaries and the two professionals assembled for the historical group photograph, thankfully preserved in the Ramsay family album and reproduced by permission of the late Freda Ramsay. Thanks are due to Past Captain Gilbert Stevenson for providing the copy negatives and enlargements of this photograph as his personal contribution to the Centenary celebrations.

Once again we are indebted to *The Scotsman* of Saturday, 23rd May 1891 for a very detailed description of the historical event, entitled :

OPENING OF THE ISLAY COURSE
MATCH BETWEEN CAMPBELL AND FERNIE

Opening of Machrie Links, 22nd May 1891

'PORT ELLEN, FRIDAY EVENING- This has been rather a notable day for Islay, in respect that it not only witnessed the formal opening for play of a golf course on the island, but it saw the fulfilment of an interesting professional fixture on the new green. A more delightful day for an open-air gathering of the kind could scarcely be imagined. All day the sun shone brightly, and the moderately fresh north-westerly breeze which blew across the island was only sufficient to temper the heat and to make the exercise of the game more exacting on the Machrie course, as the new links are named, than otherwise unpleasant.'

The writer continued to praise enthusiastically the course, the scenery and the weather. It was suggested that the match gained in interest from the fact that it was now being played over 'the one green to be found in the Hebrides'. This statement would only have been correct if it had stated 'the one 18 hole green' since 9 hole courses were opened at Stornoway in 1890 and at Askernish on South Uist in 1890/91. The Machrie Links were described as the Westward Ho of Scotland, the vast stretch of Links were compared favourably to those at Troon and Prestwick and the putting greens to those at Hoylake. Praise indeed from our correspondent obviously already smitten with the contagious golf 'disease' spreading rapidly throughout the country.

The Challenge Match - Willie Campbell v Willie Fernie

The formalities over, the Challenge match got under way. Campbell was the favourite, having laid out the course and because of his good match play reputation. The assembled gathering of ladies and gentlemen were to have their first insight into the 'royal and ancient game'. By today's standards the scoring was terrible but bearing in mind the rough condition of this new course, the preponderance of rabbit burrows and the limitations of the gutty balls and wooden shafted clubs it wasn't too bad. At first glance 39 out for both Campbell and Fernie seems pretty good until you realise it was only for eight holes. The turn in those days was the point where you physically turned round and headed back to the clubhouse. Historically, links courses occupied the narrow strip of land between the beach and arable land so that only a straight out and straight back layout was generally possible.

At the turn, Campbell was one up. Thereafter a rabbit hole, a stymie and a poor short game contributed to Fernie's 56 in 10 holes and a deficit of 5 holes. Campbell scored 89 to Fernie's 95

1st Round	Campbell	Out	5 5 3 4 4 6 5 7	= 39
		In	4 5 5 5 6 5 4 5 6 5	= 50
	Fernie	Out	6 4 4 5 4 6 5 5	= 39
		In	5 5 6 5 6 7 6 6 5 5	= 56

In the second round, in spite of Campbell falling foul of a rabbit furrow at the fifth and then losing 'The Maiden', it was not to be Fernie's day. In attempting to loft over a stymie at the seventh, he knocked Campbell's ball into the hole then fell foul of another rabbit hole at the eleventh. Campbell triumphed by 7 and 6 and was presented with the gold medal and the £100 prize-money by P.J. Mackie. Fernie, in acknowledging the three hearty cheers for the unlucky loser, stated he was willing to meet his friend Campbell again on the same course and said this was the best course he had ever seen.

Two years later Campbell joined the exodus of Scots golfers to become professionals in the USA where the game was in its infancy. After being runner up to Willie Dunn in the unofficial first USA Open in 1893 he died around the turn of the century at 38 years old.

While Willie Campbell is particularly remembered for his failure to win the 1887 Open, he did have a successful career both as a professional and course designer in Britain and the USA. He will also be remembered as the chief 'architect' of the Machrie golf course, a legacy which has been appreciated by Islay golfers in terms of the magnificent layout much of which is still in play today.

At the end of this historic day when Willie Campbell took the honours the first official General Committee Meeting was held in the club house to organise and plan the day to day running of the club. A local Committee with full powers was appointed, consisting of Major Wise, Dugald MacLeod, Lachlan McCuaig and Peter Reid who all took up their appointments as in the previously advertised committee. Peter Mackie presented his statement of income and expenditure showing a balance of £13.4s.9d. only remaining from the £170 subscribed. With only 2 members paid up in addition to the nine subscribers it was decided to postpone the Annual General Meeting. The final formality of the meeting, as noted in the Minutes, was to thank Peter Mackie:

' The meeting expressed their appreciation of the services rendered by Mr. Mackie in the formation of the club and thanked him for the vast amount of trouble he had taken in the matter.
Signed Lovat Ayshford Wise, Captain and Chairman, Islay Golf Club.'

The Islay Golf Club was off to a good start. All the desired requisites were in place and the extensive advertising campaign had been reinforced by the publicity in the press from the opening Challenge match. All that was needed now was a little patience to wait for the expected influx of golfers.

CHAPTER TWO

19th CENTURY GOWF - THE LAST DECADE

Early Days
In its early years the Islay Golf Club was to be fortunate to have several dedicated members who featured in the successful publicity campaigns and whose actions helped steer the club forward. Which direction was not immediately clear, as at this time, throughout the country there was no consistency in handicapping or in the application of the rules of golf. It was also a time of change and rapid expansion in the number of golf clubs and courses throughout Britain. Whereas there were only some 300 in 1891 the number rose dramatically to about 3,000 by 1905.

There were also major changes in the equipment being used. Gone were the long nose scared head play clubs and long and short spoons, all made by craftsmen. They were replaced by 'Bulger' drivers, brassies and spoons, accompanied by an increasing number of iron headed clubs with memorable names like cleeks, irons, mashies of many varieties, niblicks and jiggers. The poor old caddie was overburdened with the increasing number of clubs carried under his arm and so the golf bag made its appearance.

In this atmosphere of change the Islay Club got off to a slow start. Income from green fees and subscriptions was insufficient to meet the greenkeeper's wages which prompted the Club Captain, Major Wise, to subscribe another £5. The Committee considered giving the professional John Martin notice as by mid-August only 5 new members had paid up. Twenty-six people had taken out 5/- weekly tickets between July and September and hopes were high that some of them would become members. However, only another two paid their £1.1s. subscription. The expected rush of golfers to Islay had not materialised in spite of the advertising.

Early Competitions
Some competition was needed to attract the golfers and, as was the custom, a

Hugh Morrison, Captain 1892-94

gold medal was provided by the Captain for competition among members. It took place on 21st September and was won by William Ritchie from Edinburgh with a score of 108-4 =104 nett. Other nett scores included R. Ballingall (Scr)107 and Peter Reid (20) also with 107. The Minutes recorded that it was a very windy day!

One month before he completed his term of office, Major Wise, the Club Captain resigned because he was leaving the island for family reasons. He commented:

> 'I have daughters growing up and my first duty is their welfare and advantage and I feel I ought not to isolate them and shut them up here without seeing any of their fellow-kind.' !!

So Mr. Wise departed for Taunton and his landlord, Hugh Morrison of Islay Estates accepted the invitation to be Captain but this was also destined to be a relatively short appointment.

P.J. Mackie then presented a second gold medal, this time for competition by all comers, and to be played for on 27th May 1892, the same day as the Club's first A.G.M. The competition was widely advertised but the response from outside competitors was poor. Mr. G.M. Wilson from Glasgow won with a score of 104 and then joined the club. In his winning speech he offered another gold medal for future monthly competitions and expressed his opinion that the course would soon be very popular.

A minor crisis developed at this A.G.M. when the Club balance had dropped to £1.13s.7d. To encourage more members, particularly the locals, subscriptions were halved to 10/6. This wise decision produced 57 members. With a further 45 weekly tickets sold, the club was now on a more secure financial footing and it was time to attend to matters in detail.

Fixing the Handicap

Having lost the first two medals to Edinburgh and Glasgow, the local Committee decided it was time to appoint a handicap Committee, consisting of the Captain, Hugh Morrison, Doctor Gilmour, McCuaig and Reid. They fixed scratch arbitrarily at 90 from which figure all members would be handicapped. There was no universal handicap system or method of assessing the scratch score at this time so clubs more or less went their own way. The result was chaos as each club fixed their scratch score relative to the lowest scores and thus to the standard of play and the difficulty of the green. Committees were naturally aware of the visitors' potential for cleaning up the prizes. It was no different on Islay where 'strangers to

Golfing Party at Machrie, 1892 (National Museum of Scotland)

Golfers sheltering at the "Maiden", 1892 (National Museum of Scotland)

be placed at scratch or plus' and the maximum club handicap was fixed at 36. It didn't worry Mr. A. E. Orr of Ranfurly Castle Golf Club who won the July medal with a nett score of 93, i.e. 81 plus 12!!

The gap in standards between strangers such as A.E. Orr and the locals is shown by the scores of other medal winners in 1892 who were all locals.

Neil McIntyre	121-32 = 89	after a tie with Mr. Osborne	126-32=94
John Bolland	120-32 = 88	after a tie with Campbell Martin	128-36=92
J. W. Gordon	97-15 = 82	which was followed by	96-15=81

The handicapping problem was universal and the subject of much discussion in the press. *The Golfing Annual* (Vol. 8, 1893-4) gave its proposals:

'Best Plan for Handicapping'
'First fix your scratch score, i.e. average score returned for each round by your best player. Then strike a fair average for the respective scores of the other players and allow them strokes in proportion. Do not err by too liberal handicap. Limit of 18 is adequate and if scratch man improves owe him from 4 to 6 strokes - but no more.'

It was obviously written by a low handicap golfer!

As if to show what could be done, Willie Fernie returned to Islay in September 1892. He accompanied a group of well-known amateurs playing a series of matches over Troon, Machrihanish and Islay. *The Glasgow Herald* (October 3rd) reported the Islay match:

'W. Fernie playing against Mr. James Duncan of London Scottish established a record which will hold pre-eminence for a long time to come :

5 5 4 4 4 3 5 4 4 = 38 and 4 5 3 5 4 3 4 5 5 = 38 Total 76'

The arrival of Islay's first official 'bandit', Malcolm Sinclair from Port Ellen, gave the handicap Committee some problems when he scored a nett 76 off 30! The handicap problem was still around in March 1893 after the Committee had decided to fix handicaps based on the lowest score in any competition. Four days later some members arranged a meeting where a proposal by Dr. Gilmour was unanimously approved 'that an instruction be given to the handicapping Committee to reduce the maximum handicap from 36 to 30, scratch being 90'. Secretary, Peter Reid, must have been in agreement as he recorded this unofficial meeting in the Minute book. The proposal was duly approved officially but with the proviso that the medal winner would have his handicap cut by 20 per cent!

Even this rule was not strictly observed as the cuts varied from 50 per cent to 20 per cent and nil. However, some rationality was forthcoming in the treatment of 'strangers' when it was decided to accept their lowest handicap from any course but, with understandable caution, their maximum handicap was 18. The inexperienced Committee were having the same problems to resolve as those at most other recently formed golf clubs.

Early Personalities

Islay was fortunate in the high quality of the individuals who took an early interest in the development of the Golf Club. Over and above the Secretary, Peter Reid, whose praises were generally unsung, there were several others whose character and skills were ideally suited to creating the publicity which would bring the golfers to Islay.

Lachlan McCuaig - Admiral of the Port

As a founder member of Islay Golf Club and Hon. Treasurer since its inception Lachlan McCuaig appreciated early on the value of a successful golf club to the prosperity of his hotel, the White Hart, in Port Ellen and also to the community as a whole. Within a year of the opening of the course he was busy extending his hotel while, in competition, the new 'Islay Hotel' had also been built in Port Ellen, all in anticipation of a flood of golfers converging on Islay.

An excellent description of Lachlan was written by the famous Rev. John Kerr M.A. of Dirleton (of whom more later) as part of yet another article, 'Golf in Islay' as published in Volume 8 of *Golfing Annual* 1893-4:

> The best hotel at Port Ellen is undoubtedly the 'White Hart' of which an illustration is here given, from which the golfer may see how commodious and comfortable a place it is. Here is also a portrait of mine host of the 'White Hart', Mr Lachlan McCuaig. Both of these we are sure will be valued by all who have golfed at Islay, or may yet have that pleasure. With Mr McCuaig it would be well to have communication and secure a berth at the hotel before the journey is begun. This gentleman has been one of the chief promoters of golf in Islay and as he is Treasurer to the club, and takes an enthusiastic interest in the welfare and in all that concerns golf and golfers, he is the man to get hold of at the outset. His fine presence is worthy of the title he has by common consent received, 'Admiral of the Port'. He is the chief man of the place, County Councillor, School Board member, Volunteer Major, Auld Kirk elder and what not. You soon get to see how he has the confidence of everybody in the place, for he has a kind word for everybody, and a kindly regard for everything that is said or done at Port Ellen. Mr McCuaig is thoroughly versed in the history and geography of Islay, rich in humorous stories and racy anecdotes so that under his auspices a holiday here has additional delights. His chief defect is that he is a bachelor but his sister and cousin make visitors feel thoroughly at home by the way in which their comforts are attended to. If you have not the display at table that you have at

some of our big fashionable hotels, you have everything substantial and good, and the hotel is not one of the spider and fly kind, where the blood of the poor tourist is sucked during the season, the charges for everything being extremely moderate. As soon as breakfast is over, a brake pulls up at the hotel door to take golfers to the links and it returns to bring them home for dinner at 7pm. No charge is made for this drive to and from the links.As it gives one a good breath of air and a good view of the scenery, it is to some an additional charm to golf in Islay.'

Lachlan McCuaig

Sadly, he died in January 1895 before the success of the golf course and hotels was fully established. The Minutes gave him credit for the large part he played in the success of the Club since formation and stated that 'his genial manner and kindly treatment of visitors made him a general favourite and his fine figure lent charm to the golf course'. The loss of such an influential local figurehead was a severe blow to the Golf Club in its early years. Fortunately an ideal replacement was available who was an experienced golfer from the mainland and who could take up the reins and guide the club forward in the right direction.

J. S. Higginbotham

The experienced golfer arrived as a member in 1894 in the person of Mr. J. S. Higginbotham, a prominent member of the Prestwick Golf Club and a friend of

J. S. Higginbotham, Captain 1896-1906

the Ramsay family. He was a regular contributor to the golf magazines, one of his favourite subjects being the Rules. He soon had reason to question the high scratch score of the course when, off 19, he scored a nett 81, 9 under, to tie with D. MacLachlan who repeated the score in the next medal. When Treasurer ,Lachlan McCuaig died, Mr. Higginbotham was invited to join the Committee and soon he had scratch reduced to 85. If the Committee needed to be re-assured about this reduction, Alex Stuart of the New Club, Edinburgh and first winner of the Irish Amateur Championship provided the answer with a score of 79 scratch. Higginbotham quickly started to get things in order as the Rules of the Club were altered and the financial year end changed to December.

The Committee had previously obtained a copy of the St Andrews' Rules and stipulated that they should be used in the event of a disagreement over the local Rules. Higginbotham then reversed the situation when he had the St Andrews' Rules of Golf adopted at the 1896 A.G.M. but with local additions and exceptions. P.J. Mackie, the Captain, retired due to ill-health and his natural successor was Higginbotham who remained Captain for the next 10 years during which the Islay Golf Club and the Machrie Links made significant advances.

Not content with the above changes, he introduced a charge of half a crown for the use of the club house key, almost equal to 25 per cent of the annual subscription! Rules were also introduced for the 'Keeper of the Links', professionals and caddies. For example: 'When any Professional is taken out to play, he shall be paid 2/- for a round, and he paying his own Caddie.' With the Caddie's pay at 9d. for 18 holes, there wasn't much left if he failed to win the stakes on the match.

In 1897 the variable state of the handicapping system all over the country was ended when, at the request of the principal golf clubs, the R.& A. agreed to produce a standard set of rules and to be responsible for them thereafter. However, it was two years later before these new rules were adopted on Islay to be followed by a completely new set of local rules in January 1901. Mr. Higginbotham was putting his house in order, especially in preparation for the forthcoming prestigious Islay Golf tournament. There is no doubt that he was the mainstay of the Islay Golf Club at the beginning of the century and contributed greatly to its success.

Ronald McArthur - Blacksmith

When golf arrived in Islay in 1891, Ronald McArthur was the blacksmith in Port Ellen, probably with little knowledge of golf and certainly with no experience of club making. His name first appeared in the Treasurer's book in 1894 recording payment for work done by him. The bug obviously bit and he joined the Islay Golf Club. Having been given his first handicap of 30 in March the following year, he soon got into the winning way on three successive Saturdays in

Ronald MacArthur

April. First of all, he won the lamp competition with a net score of 86 which earned a reduction to 18. In the next lamp competition, a winning net 82 saw a further reduction to 14. Next came a tie on net 92 for the monthly medal followed by a net 89 to win the play off from Secretary, Peter Reid. Ronald MacArthur had started on the Islay golf scene in more ways than one. His true handicap level would appear to have been established very quickly. However, it was not the quality of his golf that brought him fame.

As golf increased in popularity and more and more golfers flocked to Islay so the demand arose for repairs to both iron and wooden clubs. The local blacksmith was the natural port of call. The magazine, *Golf*, of 27th August 1897 describes the scene:

'This worthy gentleman *yclept,* Ronald McArthur, is one of the 'institutions' of Islay, and no one should neglect while there to make his acquaintance, for Ronald is a heaven born genius in the golfing line. If your club has suffered a fracture of the skull, or any other accident, no matter how serious, you have only to commit the same to Ronald's care. Off he rides with the sufferer on his bicycle (his own make) to Port Ellen, and next day he rides up with it smiling, and you have your club as good as new, perhaps better than it was before.'

The very hard gutty ball of the time was liable to cause considerable wear on the face of the wooden clubs so Ronald developed the skill of repairing them with a leather inset.

'His 'leather faces' are so good that it is almost worthwhile to get all your clubs faced by Ronald before you leave the island. If you have a favourite which you wish a pattern of, Ronald is your man; he can in a day or two produce the article, and if anything is not quite the same depend on it the new version is the better of the two. Anything in fact from a needle to an anchor this Port Ellen genius of a blacksmith can make to order for you. Talk of patents! Why Ronald has patents the way of heads, handles, and everything else and he never registers one of them. Were he removed to larger fields of usefulness he would soon make a fortune but it would be a sorry day for Islay if Ronald left, and Ronald is too good an Islay man to think of going.'

Two years later in November 1899, we find an article in *Golf Illustrated* devoted solely to Ronald described as 'the Islay Genius who engraves views upon cleeks and irons'. A picture shows the bearded blacksmith standing with one of his trusty cleeks under his arm with the following comment:

'He was born a genius and has, unlike some other of the genius species exercised the capacity of taking pains and working for a living, and he has by the starting of Golf in Islay

A. J. Balfour

had a certain greatness thrust upon him, for he has to act as club and ball maker in the place and that without any training whatsoever. Ronald has risen to the occasion and has developed such a fine instinct for club making that he cannot supply the demands made on him for sets of manufacture, which are all made out of the ordinary, while on the iron clubs he engraves views of Islay and the surrounding islands and sea.'

His fame spread, helped by the widely advertised fact that the M.P., Hugh Morrison, had presented a set of Ronald's clubs to A. J. Balfour, then first Lord of the Treasury and later to become Prime Minister. Balfour, arguably Britain's keenest ever golfing Member of Parliament has been given the credit for the 'Scotification' of England in a golfing sense during the last two decades of the last century and beyond. When he ordered a further set of Ronald's engraved clubs and it became public knowledge, fame for the Islay genius was guaranteed. Engraving of golf clubs thus was quite unique and it was not surprising that Ronald could not meet demand.

An engraved wooden shafted putter made by McArthur is in the possession of the author. The engraving on the back has been worn off by repeated rubbing with emery paper to remove rust but there is sufficient left for the scene to be recognisable - an Islay steamer in Port Ellen with the Carraig Fhada Lighthouse, Kilnaughton Chapel and the cliffs of Oa in the background. Another engraved club is in the possession of the Islay Golf Club. It came to light rather fortuitously in a hotel bar in Gullane. Roy C. MacGregor on a golfing visit saw the club in the bar and, realising its historical importance, persuaded the owner to sell it to him for presentation to Islay Golf Club when he was elected Captain. This happened many years ago and it re-surfaced in time for the Centenary celebrations. The engraving on the back of the mashie faintly shows the Machrie House and the Oa in the background with the prominent rock formation called 'Soldiers' rock'.

Ronald was well known in golfing circles outwith the island, being regular in attendance at the Amateur Championships. Even as late as 1904 he was again the subject of a special article in *Golfing Annual* which included the picture of Ronald in full Highland dress - complete with cleek! In this article he was described by the Rev. John Kerr M.A., as quite a character, a self taught draughtsman and 'perhaps the most noted native in the place'. The engraving of the clubs was described as one of his hobbies, the artistic touch being in the family as his brother Sandy was an artist and entertaining bagpipe player. If the strains of music were heard some evenings across the waters of the bay at Port Ellen you could be sure it was Ronald and family in their boat entertaining some of the golfers from the White Hart or the Machrie.

After the initial efforts of P.J. Mackie in getting the Islay Golf Club up and running, these three characters had continued the good work, McCuaig in looking after the finances, McArthur in 'stamping' his personality on the Golf Club through his engraved clubs and Higginbotham in attending to the Rules and putting the Islay Golf Club on the right track into the next century.

Golf club made and etched by Ronald McArthur to show a steamer in Port Ellen bay and Lighthouse.

Keepers of the Green

In the last century, that majestic title 'keeper of the green' implied that maintenance of the course was the principal duty of the incumbent. He was generally a professional golfer whose duties included giving tuition and playing with members, selling and repairing clubs and balls, controlling the caddies and last but not least attending to the green, i.e. the entire course. As golf expanded rapidly towards the end of the last century and golfers demanded better conditions, the job description was abbreviated to green keeper or in some cases simply groundsman.

Prior to the official opening of the course they were simply workmen who were paid £4.16s.8d. for 'beating' the greens and erecting poles, an essential feature for golfers first setting out to find the greens amidst the hidden hollows and valleys of the links or 'machair'. Greens and fairways were rough and undefined and sheep and rabbits ensured the grass was relatively short. Punch Bowl type greens were common with their natural contours and luscious grass.

The professional John Martin only lasted five months. He was a luxury the Golf Club could not afford and his services were dispensed with from October 1891. The course was unattended during its first winter before a local man, Dugald MacDougal, was appointed 'keeper of the green' in April 1892. His salary of 13/- per week showed a big saving on Martin's £1.2s. Having worked through the winter he was eventually told in August 1893 that his services were no longer required because 'he was not qualified as a greenkeeper'.

His successor was John McMillan from Port Ellen who was heading for a long and successful career at the Machrie. Presumably he was qualified probably as a gardener or groundsman. His authority over the caddies was confirmed by an alteration to the club rules to the effect that 'caddies must tee the ball in the ground marked by the greenkeeper and must obey his orders'.

Rabbits, four-legged variety, were creating havoc and Peter Reid wrote to the 'shooting tenant' asking if the club could trap rabbits on the line of the course after normal trapping time had expired. Permission was granted on condition that the trapped rabbits were given to the tenant!

McMillan's starting wage was 14/- per week which rose to 18/- five years later after a written request for an increase. To satisfy the ongoing demand for better playing conditions the Committee decided to purchase a second hand horse mower for £24.10s. and to get the lawnmower put in good order. As an afterthought it was also decided to get costs for a horse. Obviously the sheep were not keeping the grass short enough! McMillan was obviously proving satisfactory, playing a bit of golf and even qualified for a mention in the numerous golf magazines. 'McMillan the green-keeper promises well to attain distinction as a player, cultivating the game in his spare hours without neglecting his other duties.' He played several matches against J. Currie from Gullane who had competed successfully for Oxford v Cambridge. Mr. Currie, conceding one third lost all the matches.

The first steps had been taken by the greenkeeper towards recognition as a professional. At least *The Daily Mail* thought so in an article on the Islay Golf Course in July 1899, commenting that 'John McMillan, the greenkeeper and professional plays a good game and gets around in almost scratch' which then was 82. Two years later, playing in the Islay Golf Tournament, he had made the grade when he was quoted as the local professional.

Peter Jeffrey Mackie of Lagavulin,
Captain 1894-96.

Lagavulin Quaich, presented by P. J. Mackie in 1894.

From the Visitors' Book

The golf explosion of the late 19th century produced the regular publication of magazines and books devoted exclusively to golf. Some poems on golf were also included and the Machrie Links was a natural subject.

The magazine, *Golf,* of August 1897, records possibly the earliest poem on golf on the Machrie Links along with some candid comments and a challenge to golfers to improve on the effort:

'The Visitors' Book at Machrie contains the names of many distinguished golfers who have paid a visit to this famous Golf course and given a verdict in its favour. One who is too modest to give his name bursts into rhyme, but only to prove that Golf, with all its attractions, is not a subject for poetry. When we append the following lines, it will be seen that a grand opportunity is open to some golfing poet to do justice to this noble course:-

I'll tee my ball on Machrie Links,
By Laggan's sounding strand,
For nature sure designed this course
As a golfer's happy land.

A fairer prize has ne'er inspired
To doughty deeds I we'en
Than Scotsman's Maiden, fairest wench,
But coy as e'er was seen.

Strong is his arm and clear his eye
Who gains this lovely prize,
Out of the Punch Bowl he may pledge
A toast to her bright eyes.

After the depths of dark Ifrinn,
What pleasure 'tis to turn
To Mount Zion's Elysian heights,
Despite the dreaded burn.

After the Grave is safely past,
A time that surely shall come,
We'll homeward gladly wend our way
To meet a Highland welcome.'

Comments following this poem refer to the new situation that golfers found on Islay including:

'If he wishes to purchase some new golf balls he will call on the doctor at Port Ellon, who keeps the same, like his pills, in stock.'

This could refer to Dr. T. F. Gilmour who was a Committee member at this time. The poem may be his and if so his poetry was on par with his golf as in 1898 he won Mrs. Ramsay's spoon(wooden) for scores of 137 and 106 - Nett! What is more certain is that he took up the golf correspondent's challenge, albeit eleven years later. (see next chapter)

The 19th Hole

The clubhouse of the Islay Golf Club has since the beginning been a small corrugated iron or timber structure used mainly as changing and locker rooms. The traditional 19th hole image of the Machrie Hotel really developed from 1899 when a re-arrangement of the course brought the 1st tee and 18th green adjacent to the hotel.

The late Mrs. Freda Ramsay provided most of the historical data relating to the

Iain Ramsay

Golfers arrive at Machrie Hotel, early this century.

Bert Marshall.

John MacIntyre Snr, Captain 1987-88 with Ralph Middleton (r), Hon. Secretary 1959-71.

Max McGill, Captain 1987-88 about to drive himself into office.

early days of the Machrie Hotel or Machrie House as it was first known. The data came from the Sederunt Book of Kildalton and the Machrie House and Machrie Farm Rentals.

The farm at Machrie was developed in the 1880s and the farmhouse was completed late in the decade before golf at Machrie was thought about. A few months after the opening of the Machrie golf course, John Ramsay of Kildalton saw the potential and decided to convert the farmhouse to a guest house for the golfers. He put his cook and housekeeper of many years, Miss Ann McPhee, in as manageress and extended the house during the winter of 1891-1892. Before it was finished he sadly passed away and, as his son Iain was only 14 years old, the estate was put in the hands of a trustee, James Badenoch Nicholson of Glenbervie. He visited Machrie in April 1892 and approved expenditure of £480 on the extension because of Mr. Ramsay's previous communications to the effect that the establishment of the golf course constituted a valuable estate improvement.

The reliable and successful manageress decided to get married, became Mrs. Bell and promptly lost her job as, with a typical Victorian attitude, 'her services can no longer be called upon'. Lachlan McCuaig stepped in smartly and took over the let of both house and farm at £200 per annum for 5 years. The lease conditions stated that 'two stalls in the stables be reserved for the estate, the right to the Golf Course be reserved and keep the House open for the accommodation of golfers'.

The extension was an immediate success with House full notices up during July and August. The charge for boarders was £2.5s. per week which brought the season's income to £232.10s. against expenditure of £141.18s.1d.

After the death of Mr. McCuaig in 1895, trustees were again involved before the lease was transferred in 1896 to his sisters Isobella and Annie but their tenancy was short. Having bought the White Hart they decided to concentrate their efforts on it and gave up the lease of the Machrie House and farm in favour of Miss Jessie Mackay in 1900. Fate and circumstances had dictated that she was the fourth person to manage the Machrie House in ten years. With a 15 year lease she would be hoping that the new century would give her the chance to show some continuity in the management of the Machrie.

The Lagavulin Challenge Quaich

One of the most important contributions to the competitive life of the club in the 1890s was the presentation of a magnificent silver trophy by Peter J. Mackie in 1894, the year he was elected Captain. Mackie, of Lagavulin Distillery, had realised that in the early years of its development the club needed to attract the top golfers to Islay and to ensure their return in future years. In 1894 when he presented the trophy, to be known as the Lagavulin Challenge Quaich, no doubt he envisaged it would have a long life on Islay. He had taken over as Captain from Hugh Morrison of Islay Estates who had resigned because, as an M.P. in England, 'he did not find Islay very convenient for meetings'.

The competition rules for the Lagavulin Challenge Quaich were set by Mr Mackie viz.- best nett score over one round of the Links, club members only eligible to compete and the Quaich to become the property of anyone winning for the third time. Five miniature replicas were also provided for the winners.

The first winner on 25th September 1894 was John Bolland with a score of 105-14=91. Unfortunately he had to wait until the following January before the cup arrived for presentation! It was a good year for him as he also won a set of clubs and a bag presented by A.T. Hay of Ardbeg. Mr. Hay was another prominent figure in the whisky industry and was an original subscriber to the Golf Club. His death was recorded at the A.G.M. of 1896 as one 'who always had an active interest in the Club'.

The Committee may have had some cause to regret the three winner rule in 1899. Golfers G.M. Orr and H.C. Cameron had two wins each and the stage seemed set for a battle to gain the Quaich for keeps. Surprisingly Orr did not defend his title as holder and it was left to Cameron to take the Quaich and his third replica back to the mainland. He and his father, Sir H.C. Cameron M.D., who was a well kent figure in Scottish golfing circles were both regular visitors to Machrie, and friends of the Ramsay family.

However, the tale of the Lagavulin Quaich does not end there. John McIntyre Snr., provided the story of how it resurfaced some 72 years later. About 1971-2, Joe Soutter, who had been Captain in 1968/9, received a phone call from a friend in London saying he had located one of the Islay Golf Club trophies which had been stolen in 1968. He promptly headed for London only to find it wasn't one of the missing trophies but the Lagavuln Quaich which had been put up for auction by a grand-daughter of H.C. Cameron. End of story? Not by a long way.

Just after Centenary year the writer saw on display in the Burrell Gallery in Glasgow an imposing large silver quaich in a glass case. It was the Lagavulin Quaich! The inscription round the rim read, 'Lagavulin Challenge Quaich presented by the Captain, 1894, Peter Jeffrey Mackie'. Islay Golf Club is inscribed round the base and the only winner's name given is that of John Bolland. The most striking feature is the detailed engraved golfing scene showing a gentleman golfer in knickerbocker suit at the top of his backswing, another in Norfolk jacket, a caddie with clubs under his arm and a group of spectators in the background. It is a magnificent example of craftsmanship, correct in all detail and gives a true pictorial history of golf at that time. The design was by Elkington of London.

Henry Cotton with "Cross" winner A. MacFarlane and runner up.

The Kildalton Cross and Machrie Hotel.

Appetite whetted, with help from Brian Morrison of Morrison Bowmore Distillers, the writer was put in touch with Gordon McIntosh a director of Keepers of the Quaich which keeps us on the whisky trail. The Keepers of the Quaich is an exclusive international society founded by the principal Scotch whisky distillers. Its objectives are to honour people worldwide who by deed or speech have recognised 'the nobility of Scotch' a product which is 'influential and fundamental to the way of life in Scotland'.

McIntosh, then employed by White Horse Distillers, revealed that years ago after the London auction the Lagavulin Quaich again resurfaced when it was offered to him,. He promptly bought it on behalf of the company for the princely sum of £120. The seller obviously thought they would probably have a bit more cash available than the golf club! The Quaich then returned to the golf game in 1980 when a new plinth was added for the inauguration of a prestigious new tournament, the Licensed Trade Invitational Team Golf Championship. Like the original competition it also survived for five years and the Quaich is now displayed in the entrance to the White Horse Distillers head office in Shieldhall, Glasgow. Having now travelled the full circle to be back where it started in P.J. Mackie's Company, perhaps some day the Quaich might take another step forward to its rightful home at the Islay Golf Club. (See Postscript, Newsflash 2.) The original winners and their scores were as follows:-

```
1894   John Bolland    105 -14        = 91
       (Competition extended to 36 holes in 1895)
1895   G. M. Orr       98+ 88 -18     = 168
1896   H.C. Cameron    99+101 -26     = 174
1897   H.C. Cameron    102+ 92 -18    = 176
       in play off after tie with
       R. B. Kennedy   101+ 94 -18    = 177
1898   G.M. Orr        87+ 88 - 8     = 167
1899   H.C. Cameron    93+ 93 - 4     = 182
```

Even at this late date it would be good to see all winners' names engraved on the Quaich.

John Bolland was the only local winner of the Lagavulin Quaich. When he retired in March 1914 after 17 years as Hon. Treasurer of the Islay G.C., a cake and wine banquet was held in his honour at the Machrie Hotel. *The Oban Times* recorded the occasion in detail:

'His close friend, golfing partner and fellow Committee member, Donald Osborne, presented him, with a well filled purse of sovereigns, the spontaneous gift of his golfing comrades. Relating reminiscences of their golfing, Mr Osborne remembered walking from Machrie on the day of the opening match between Fernie and Campbell. That was the first game of golf either of them had ever seen and both agreed in seeing very little of the pastime. Within a year's time they both had the golfing fever.'

The Evening Times Trophy

The ninth tournament for the Evening Times Trophy was played at Troon in September 1899 when an Islay G.C. team of A.C. Robertson and I. M. Walker achieved fame for the club. In previous years the tournament was completely dominated by east coast golfers. On this occasion for the first time ever a foursome team from the west reached the final. Islay disposed of Irvine, Kinghorn, Oban and Alexander by 7 and 5, 6 and 5, 7 and 5, and 3 and 1 respectively before facing the favourites Edinburgh University in the semi-final. They then battled through gales, rain and hail to win 1 up and face the Western Club from Gailes in the final. Unfortunately Islay lost but it was a fine effort and almost certainly the first success abroad!

As the end of the century approached the Islay Golf Club was in good order with the handicapping system and the rules having been rationalised. Captain Higginbotham was at the helm and receiving continued support from P.J. Mackie and the Ramsay family. Although the prestigious Lagavulin Quaich had departed plans were afoot for a replacement trophy and for an ambitious tournament guaranteed to bring Islay golf to the notice of all golfers throughout Britain.

CHAPTER THREE

DAWN OF A NEW CENTURY

The Islay Golf Club was not without a major trophy for long. Two months after the departure of the Lagavulin Quaich, the generosity of the Ramsay family again came to the rescue when Mrs. Ramsay offered to present a replacement in the form of a silver Challenge Kildalton Cross. Acceptance was unanimous and immediate as was the reaction to Iain Ramsay's offer of £100 as first prize in an open tournament to be held at Machrie. With changes to the course and the relocation of the clubhouse in the pipeline, Islay golf was about to take a gigantic leap forward into the 20th century.

The Kildalton Cross
The 9th century Kildalton High Cross in the churchyard of the Kildalton Chapel is one of the finest examples of ancient carved stones in Scotland. It is closely related to those on Iona and has well preserved intricate carving in local bluestone. John Ramsay of Kildalton had a great interest in preserving Islay's antiquities and when the Cross was leaning over dangerously he arranged for it to be reset on a stable foundation under the supervision of the Society of Antiquities. He was an intelligent practical man involved in politics, as M.P. for Falkirk, in shipping and distilling. He had a deep love for Scotland and its people with a special interest in education both practically and politically. He was responsible for building schools in Islay and other islands and in many cases he paid the schoolmaster's salary. In recognition of his saving of the Cross, the Scottish Society of Antiquities presented him with a magnificent silver replica of the Kildalton Cross. Thus when the subject of a replacement for the Lagavulin Quaich arose, his widow, Lucy Ramsay quickly offered a replica Kildalton cross in silver. She would not have realised how influential it would be in contributing substantially to the future success of the Golf Club and the Machrie Links. The first competition for the Cross was held in 1900 but the full story comes later.

Enticing the Professionals to Islay

In December 1899, Mr. Higginbotham informed his Committee that Mr. Iain Ramsay had offered to give £100 as the first prize in an open tournament at Machrie. The Club members were to be invited to subscribe towards the other prizes which would be at least £20 to the runner up and £10 each to the other semi-finalists. However, it was in *Golf Illustrated* of 7th July the following year that their Ayr correspondent first broke the news that something extraordinary was planned for Islay in 1901:

> 'If somebody does not anticipate them, the Machrie Golf Club are going to create a record in tournaments.......it is in this Elysium that it is proposed to arrange probably the most imposing tournament ever held in the history of golf'.

Although the total prize money wasn't stated at this time the emphasis on the value of the first prize led to the competition being publicised as the 'Islay £100 Tournament'. The article continued: 'no such prize has ever hitherto been played for in a tournament.'

In the continuing campaign to publicise the Machrie and the Islay Golf Club, this was undoubtedly the most ambitious proposal to date. If there had been any doubts in the minds of the Committee they would soon be erased by the thought that success must be guaranteed by the attraction of a first prize which was 4 times greater than that for the Open. In fact it was to be 45 years later before the Open first prize exceeded £100.

For some time prior to the tournament, changes were being made to the course and extensions were being planned for Machrie House. Prior to 1900 the clubhouse was situated towards Kintra with the first and 18th holes reasonably adjacent. In December 1899 it was decided that the round should start and finish at Machrie House. This meant the clubhouse had to be moved so the proprietor was asked to build a new one at the first tee. Not surprisingly, considering the recent generosity of the Ramsay family, the request was turned down and Ronald McArthur was given the contract to move the existing one to its new location at a cost of £12. It was possibly extended as the final sum paid was £19.8s.6d. McArthur boasted that the work was done 'without a single pane of glass being broken'.

Once again for most of the professionals the impending trip to Islay would be a journey into the unknown. Some idea of the adventure ahead could be gleamed from the earlier *Golf* magazine of April 1898 in an article describing the alternative journey by the steamer 'Islay' from Greenock to Port Ellen via the Mull of 'Cantyre':

'It is a journey of about 8 hours from Greenock and it is worth the extra time. The accommodation is good and the scenery, for the better part of the route is some of the most varied and spectacular in the Western Isles of Scotland. You may find for your companions a contingent of Gaelic speaking shepherds or farmers bringing flocks of prize sheep, in charge of careful, undemonstrative collies, from Glasgow or Greenock, or a few sportsmen on shooting bent on Islay or some island further north. The ordinary tourist or tripper is not much in evidence. In the steerage portion of the vessel one may find a dozen farm servants of both sexes returning home who, to relieve the tedium of the journey, when night closes in and the moon comes out improvise reels and strathspeys on deck to the stirring strains of the violin. Everywhere one hears no language except the Gaelic, the sailors speak it, the shepherds argue about the price and condition of their flocks in it and the lovers whisper it. When the moon appears, casting its tremulous streams of light on the waves, the outline of the mountains dimly revealed, and the headland light thrown athwart the path of the steamer, the scene is one of the most memorable the golfer on health and pleasure bent can wish to enjoy.'

Once ashore the writer continues:

'On all sides one hears nothing but Gaelic. As far as the English language is concerned one may be in a foreign land. Yet these Western Highlanders, like the Welsh, are bi-lingual. Gaelic and English are compulsory in schools and the population are keen and intelligent speaking English with a slightly archaic idiom and foreign intonation which is very charming to the ear.'

Only after having finished extolling the virtues of Islay and its people does the writer get round to describing the golf course and its personalities. The journey for the professionals would not be quite so idyllic.

The Great Triumvirate

At the turn of the century, James Braid, John Henry Taylor and Harry Vardon were simply known as the best professionals of their time. It was some years later before the golf writers, reminiscing on their domination of golf over some 20 years, penned the description 'The Great Triumvirate'. Their origins were quite diverse, Braid from Earlsferry in Fife, Taylor from Northam in Devon and Vardon from Grouville in Jersey. They had two things in common; all came from a working class family and all were brought up in a prime golfing environment.

Braid was an apprentice joiner in an area where the coastline was littered with golf courses and clubmakers. By his mid teens he was a scratch golfer. After working in St. Andrews and Edinburgh he moved to London in 1893 as club maker to the famous Army and Navy Stores. When he arrived in 1901 for the Islay Golf Tournament it was as Open Champion, having won for the first time at

The Great Triumvirate at opening of a 9 hole extension to West Wilts Golf Course in 1907.
l. to rt. - J. H. Taylor, James Braid, A. J. Balfour and Harry Vardon.

Muirfield the previous week with Vardon second and Taylor third. Braid's peak years were 1901 to 1910 when he won his five Open titles.

Taylor known latterly as 'J.H.' came from a labourer's family living near Westward Ho, the home of the Royal North Devon Golf Club, where having left school at 10 he became a full time caddie. This was the first seaside links course in England and it was appropriate that 'J.H.' was the first English born professional to win the Open in 1894, the first time it was held in England. Taylor took much longer than Braid to achieve his 5 Open titles between 1894 and 1913.

Vardon was brought up on the fringe of the Royal Jersey golf course. He worked as a gardener before deciding to join brother Tom in England to become a professional golfer. In 1900 he travelled throughout the U.S.A. promoting a new guttie ball, the Vardon Flyer. While there he won the U.S.A. Open from 'J.H.' who was also on tour promoting the sale of his golf clubs. Vardon did much to publicise golf in the U.S.A. but did little for the Flyer as within a year the 'Haskell' rubber cored ball had arrived and gutties quickly went into history. His 6 Open wins were spread over 18 years from 1896 to 1914, a record which modern golfers are still trying to emulate.

The above résumé illustrates the quality of golfers who were expected to be enticed over to Islay all looking to win the £100 first prize.

The Islay £100 Tournament

The tournament was advertised as offering the highest ever first prize in an open stroke play tournament, although greater sums had been played for in the popular challenge matches between leading professionals. It was scheduled to begin on Wednesday 12th June 1901 but most of the players, having come straight from the Open at Muirfield, arrived on the Monday. The person least looking forward to the sail to Islay would be Braid who was a bad traveller with a fear of the sea which originated from his many golfing trips across the Forth from Fife to Edinburgh. In a particularly rough passage round the Mull, Braid apparently spent the entire journey flat on his back oblivious to his surroundings. Tuesday was practice day when Braid and his like threw off the worst effects of the journey.

The foremost golfers of the day were all there including Braid, the Open Champion, and ex-Champions Taylor, Vardon and Willie Fernie. Other notables present were 'Andra' Kirkaldy, Tom Vardon, Ben Sayers, Sandy Herd and Jack White. The last two were also due to become Open Champions within the next 3 years. At the last moment the famous amateur champion and twice Open Champion, Harold H.

Hilton called off otherwise the first six in the previous Open would all have been present. The favourites were the triple Open winners Taylor and Vardon. With everything ready for the greatest two days in the history of the Machrie and the Islay Golf Club great praise was given to Higginbotham and his Committee but unfortunately the club President, Iain Ramsay, was absent on call of duty in the Boer War in South Africa.

The format was the popular match play. With 32 names in the first round draw the professionals were matched against the amateurs and a new draw was planned for the second round. *The Scotsman's* golf correspondent, still a devoted fan of the Machrie Links described the scene at the start:

> 'A group of caddies, barefooted many of them and bonnet-less and all chattering in Gaelic, awaited the players in front of the Machrie House. From among these Donalds, Ronalds, Dougalds, Malcolms and Anguses, Harry Vardon selected a sturdy little bare-legged chap, whose head barely reached to the band of the professional's jacket. There were comparatively few spectators about when the first round was started at half past ten o'clock and it was difficult to imagine that prizes to the value of £170 were at stake. Indeed one is forcibly reminded of the conditions sometimes pending a boxing engagement when the fighters retire to some distant island to 'have it out' in presence only of their seconds and bottle holders.'

First Round Results

Harry Vardon, Ganton	bt Mr.A. Riley, Glasgow Western G.C.*	by 9 & 7
J. H. Taylor, Richmond	bt Mr.G. Hogg, Manchester	by 5 & 4
Jack White, Seaford	bt Mr. Gemmell, Bogside	by 6 & 4
A. Herd, Huddersfield	bt Mr.A.M. McAdam, Pollock *	by 7 & 6
Tom Vardon, Sandwich	bt Mr.P.D. Hendry, Bogside *	by 9 & 7
R. O. Dallmeyer, Manchester	bt John McMillan, Islay	by 5 & 3
W. Fernie, Troon	bt Mr. W. Laidlaw, Troon *	by 3 & 2
A. Kirkaldy, St Andrews	bt Mr. Rintoul, Milngavie	by 6 & 5
J. Kinnell, Norwich	bt R. McArthur, Islay retired	
A. Tingey, West Herts	bt M. H. Williams, Portrush	by 7 & 6
Ralph Smith, West Middlesex	bt Mr. T. D. Cummins, North Wales	by 3 & 2
Mr.T. Stevenson, Troon*	walked over, T. G. Renouf, Silloth	absent
Ben Sayers, N. Berwick	bt Mr.E. D. Evans, Islay	by 5 & 3
Tom Yeoman, Frinton	bt Neil Smith, Islay	by 2 & 1
Mr.W. A. Lambie, Glasgow Western G.C.*	walked over, Mr.H.H. Hilton	absent
James Braid, Romford	bt Mr. A. Dunlop, Bogside	by 8 & 7

Note (1) As was the custom of the time amateurs were referred to as 'Mr.'.
(2) Those marked with an asterisk were also members of Islay G.C.

Caddies, early this century. l to rt. Standing, Iain MacIntyre, Duncan Morrison, Seated Peter Carmichael and Alex MacIntyre.

The first round draw, having been seeded, became partly an Islay versus the Rest of Britain match. Messrs. Lambie and Evans, winners-to-be of the Kildalton Cross in 1902 and 1903 were perhaps the best of the Islay players. Neil Smith, described as the other Islay professional, was probably the assistant greenkeeper to John McMillan. Smith's match was the closest of the Islay players but the expected massacre of the amateurs duly took place.

In the second round, Mr. Lambie, a scratch golfer from the Glasgow Western golf course in Ruchill, Glasgow, gave the best performance of the Islay players when he only lost to Jack White on the 17th green. With other members of his family he had been a member of Islay G.C. for four years and was a well known footballer, formerly with Queens Park Football Club. He put his local knowledge to good use and 'putting in splendid style' gave White a very close contest. It was a fine performance against a professional who had just finished 6th in the Open and 4th and 2nd in the two previous ones.

Second Round Results

Taylor	bt Fernie	by 3 & 1
H. Vardon	bt Sayers	by 3 & 2
Kinnell	bt Mr.T. Stevenson	by 6 & 5
Herd	bt Yeoman	by 4 & 3
Smith	bt T. Vardon	by 2 & 1
Kirkaldy	bt R. O. Dallmeyer	by 3 & 1
Braid	bt Tingey	by 4 & 3
White	bt Mr. W.A. Lambie	by 2 & 1

The draw had ensured that two of the triumvirate could meet in the finals. However, a similar intriguing match was guaranteed in the third round between Taylor and Harry Vardon. The few spectators present were not disappointed. In spite of a half gale and heavy rain which dictated no umbrellas and waterproofs from head to foot, they were treated to an enthralling contest of magnificent golf. *The Scotsman's* correspondent reported:

'Seldom in the history of the game has a more exciting finish been seen than that today between the two English professionals and the few people who were on the course had good reason for declaring that it was well worth their while having come to the distant island to see that finish.'

The infamous 405 yards long Mount Zion featured prominently all week and was rarely conquered. Fernie took 8 the previous day and Vardon had his third successive 6 to go one down to Taylor. By the turn he was 2 down to Taylor's 40 out. Still 2 down and 3 to play his cause seemed hopeless. A win was encouraging at the 16th followed by another at the next after Taylor 'foozled' his approach to the green. Fine 3's at the 18th saw them all square with Taylor round in 83 to Vardon's 81, so down the 19th they went. The gallery increased. The elements eased off as if with respect to the famous contestants and this historic duel. The scoring improved. Taylor after a weak run up holed a 5 yard putt at the 19th to get a half. The next was halved in 4 after Vardon's long putt from the edge of the green sat on the lip. They headed for Mount Zion where a decision seemed inevitable. Both reached the 'tableland' in 3. Vardon holed his tricky 5 yard downhill putt for a 4. "It's all over," thought the spectators, but Taylor, renowned for his match play, dropped his 4 yard putt for another half. 'If the applause which followed was not loud because of lack of numbers it was none the less hearty on that account', reported *The Scotsman.* After another half in 4 at the next it again seemed all over at the 23rd when Vardon's 'tee stroke' finished in a 'nasty furrow' and he had to be content with a 'half stroke out'. Meanwhile Taylor, home in two, was left with a 4 foot putt for the match. He took his time and someone was heard to say, "£100 lies on that bit of sward between ball and hole." He missed and showed his disgust. Both reached the 24th green in 3 with Vardon 4 feet away and Taylor 3 feet away. Yet another half seemed inevitable as Vardon putted short but left Taylor a stymie. The Scotsman described the climax:

'The slope of the green, however, favoured the Richmond professional, and playing the stroke with fine precision, he ran the ball past that of his opponent and into the hole, thus winning the match after one of the most exciting finishes ever witnessed in a golf competition.'

	Third round results
Taylor	bt H. Vardon at 24th
Herd	bt Kinnell by 2 holes
A. Kirkaldy	bt C.R. Smith by 1 hole
Braid	bt White at 19th

All the games were closely contested as they all went to the 18th or beyond. A hole in one by Herd at the 205 yards Punch Bowl hardly merited a mention as if it was an everyday affair. This is surprising since with no short holes under 200 yards the records don't even show any holes in two, and even 3's were a rarity.

As the tournament progressed the barefooted caddies seem to have been dispensed with or perhaps rounded up by the school master. Ronald McArthur

John MacMillan
Greenkeeper/Professional

Mount Zion

48

described as the 'genius of the island' caddied for 'Andra' Kirkaldy in his semi-final match against the Open Champion. The others also had fellow professionals as caddies. The weather improved greatly for the afternoon round. Kirkaldy's cause seemed lost when he was 4 down with 6 to play but thanks to his caddie's good advice and missed 3 and 2 feet putts by Braid he was only one down after 16. However, a good four at Ifrinn saw Braid safely into the final.

Taylor, perhaps feeling the effects of his marathon morning match, took 44 to the turn to be one down to Herd's 42. Two holes later he was 2 down before he produced some spectacular golf. A win at the thirteenth was followed by a 10 yard putt for a half at the next, a long putt holed from the edge of the green at the next and finally a holed mashie approach to the 16th. A good 4 at Machrie was enough to see Taylor safely into the 36 hole final against his great rival - a match comparable in modern times to an Open play off between Nicklaus and Watson when at their peak.

Next morning, as the two golfing gladiators arrived in the arena for the final they were relieved to find the weather had abated further. Not a speck was visible in the clear blue sky with no wind. *The Scotsman* was again to the fore in fully reporting the final which was to be over 36 holes:

> 'It was a great day for Islay, and in honour of the occasion the children from Port Ellen were given a half-holiday that they might help to augment the little party that stood by the gate of Machrie farm-house when Braid and Taylor appeared.'

The school's attitude to golf had certainly changed from that of several years earlier when an entry in the school log book stated 'a large number of boys were absent today being employed, in some cases illegally, as caddies'. The change of heart was understandable as the headmaster, Donald MacLachlan, had become an enthusiastic golfer and could be present without any guilty conscience.

The match started at 10.30am, two Open Champions battling over 36 holes for the largest first prize in history to date in any open tournament and, as a bonus, Scotland v England as well. Could Braid, having won successive tournaments at Musselburgh and Muirfield make it three in a row? The script could not have been written any better.

The spectators, all 30 of them, saw an exciting start, when Braid famous for his long driving, put his drive into the bunker just short of the green at the 1st hole (265 yards), failed to get fully out and then holed his mashie pitch for a 3 to win the hole. His booming drive at the next was 30 yards ahead of Taylor but he still halved in 4. Mount Zion (405 yards) gave Braid a chance to show his power. *The Scotsman* noted that 'the usual mode of reaching the green is by two strokes with a play club(driver) and a pitch'. Braid just failed to make the plateau green with his mashie-iron (about a 4 iron) second and matched Taylor's orthodox 5. Then disaster for Braid at the 4th. Putting for a winning 4 from 3 yards he was over strong and his ball curled behind Taylor's to lay himself a nasty stymie which he failed to negotiate. Thanks to Taylor's 3 yard putt at the Maiden he reached the turn all square, both 40 to the turn.

Braid started home in determined fashion when his long brassie second to Manipur set up a winning 3. His cleek shot to the Punch Bowl was superior to Taylor's driver but they still halved in 3. Taylor squared at the 13th, halved the next and lost the 15th, Druim, after putting badly. His perfect 4 at the 16th (Ifrinn) squared the match with both round in 79.

Braid	out	3 4 5, 6 4 6, 4 3 5	= 40	
	in	3 5 3, 5 4 5, 5 5 4	= 39	Total 79
Taylor	out	4 4 5, 5 4 5, 4 4 5	= 40	
	in	4 5 3, 4 4 6, 4 5 4	= 39	Total 79

In the afternoon Braid's suspect putting saw him one down after missing from 2 feet at the 2nd but by the 7th he was again one up. His long driving gave him the advantage at the 8th hole (Lag) which he birdied in the morning. Expectancy was high among the spectators knowing that the record of two for this hole was held by Ronald McArthur who was heard to mutter, "Jist afraid that Braid might beat it." He didn't, but won with an easy 4. A half in 6 at the Scotsman's Maiden saw him 2 up with 9 to play and the favourite. However, Taylor wasn't giving in yet. The turning point came immediately at the tenth where Taylor laid Braid a difficult stymie which he failed to overcome with his lofting iron. Braid missed from 5 feet at the next to go back to all square again. Both made errors in the remaining holes such that only 2 holes were halved in the last 8 holes. The golf was perhaps disappointing for these two great players but was exciting for the spectators as the match stood all square on the last tee. Braid pulled his tee shot into rough country, had difficulty in getting clear and faced up to a ten yard putt for a half. The late Alastair Shanks, as part of his contribution to the history, relates the story passed on by his father:

'There was a prize of £100 on offer (a large sum in those days) and the distinction of the prize hinged on a final putt which was making straight for the hole when it was deflected by a sheep's dropping. One of the local spectators was heard to whisper in an awe-struck voice (apparently it sounds better in Gaelic)- only a sheep's dropping between him and £100!'

The Scotsman described the putt: 'Braid got the line nicely, the ball striking the back of the disc and bounding out.' It had been an uphill fight all the way for Taylor but his more consistent golf over the last nine holes earned him the first prize. Braid's consolation was £40, Herd and Kirkaldy £10 each and the defeated quarter finalists £2.10s. each.

Approximate scores

Braid	out	4 5 5 3 5 5 4 4 6	= 41	
	in	5 6 3 4 6 6 5 4 5	= 44	Total 85
Taylor	out	4 4 5 4 5 5 5 5 6	= 43	
	in	4 5 4 4 4 5 5 5 4	= 40	Total 83

Clearly the more consistent player had come out on top. Whereas Braid had six 3's and six 6's over the 36 holes, the winner had only one 3 and two 6's. Unfamiliarity and course difficulty contributed to the high scoring which relates to the scratch score of 85. Harry Vardon showed what could be achieved by scoring 76 that week as recorded in the Minutes as 4 4 5, 5 5 5, 4 4 4(40) and 4 5 4, 4 4 4, 5 3 3(36).

Undoubtedly, this unprecedented tournament finally put the Islay Golf Club and the Machrie Links on the golfing map of Scotland. Publicity was extensive in all newspapers and golf journals. Not surprisingly, the Islay Golf Club made a loss on this brave venture. Captain Higginbotham, MacBraynes and Mr. Hay of Ardbeg Distillery all donated £10 towards the total prize fund collected of £179.12s.6d., of which £170 was paid out in prizes. After deduction of expenses for advertising, extra labour and hospitality, the total loss was £10.15s.3d. The members rallied round and covered the loss as three of them promptly paid five guineas each to become life members.

The professionals were well catered for. Eight of the 13 visiting professionals received a prize, the club had negotiated cheap steamer tickets from MacBrayne and with typical Islay hospitality, £6.8s. of the prize fund surplus was spent on refreshments for them. They had no time to linger on Islay as next morning Braid, Taylor and Harry Vardon, along with Willie Fernie, were due at Bogside for another series of matches over 36 holes. The leading professionals of this period were constantly on the move earning their keep from mainly challenge or exhibition matches. Three days later Braid, Taylor, Herd and Andrew Kirkaldy were booked in for a 36 holes series at Blackhill, Glasgow, the home at that time of the Glasgow Golf Club. Like Islay this was the Club's most prestigious event to date. Tee off times were fixed for 3.00pm and 6.00pm to suit the office workers who turned out in numbers slightly greater than Islay - approximately 3000!

Such was the life of the leading professional golfers at the turn of the century. Bearing in mind the long time spent in travelling between venues, they lived a pretty hectic life. Their visit to Machrie certainly contributed to the future prosperity of the Machrie and the Islay G.C. Now nearly 100 years on, if some philanthropic golfing entrepreneur could persuade the likes of Norman, Faldo, Lyle and Montgomery to fly Loganair for a televised match on Islay, both the Machrie and the Islay G.C. would receive another boost to their prosperity. If not soon, how about June 2001?

Rev. John Kerr, M.A. F.R.S.E. F.S.A. Scot - Minister of Dirleton

Much of the credit for the success of the early publicity campaigns spreading the gospel about the delights of Machrie golf course can be attributed to the pen of the Rev. John Kerr from Dirleton, East Lothian. He was a dedicated golfer, captivated by the Machrie Links and the people of Islay as illustrated by his several articles in golf journals spanning 10 years from 1894.

He wrote extensively on golf and his other pastime, curling, recording for future generations the history of these sports. In fact, his books have become very valuable for reference and much sought after as collector's items. *The History of Curling*, published in 1890, was his first major publication. It began as a history of his club, the Royal Caledonian Curling Club, before expanding into the sport in general. Later in 1902, as chaplain to the Royal Caledonian Curling Club, Kerr was much involved in discussions and letters in *The Scotsman* concerning the proposal to send, for the first time, a Scottish Curling team to Canada and the U.S.A. His enthusiasm saw him appointed Captain of the team which made the trip in the winter 1902-3. The opportunity for another book arose and with the information supplied by local historians it was eventually published in 1904, a massive volume of 788 pages entitled *Curling In Canada and The United States.*

Kerr's ambition had been to do for golf what he had already done for curling but he didn't quite make it and had to settle for *The Golf Book of East Lothian.* This magnificent treatise was published in 1894 and dedicated to Arthur J. Balfour, a future Prime Minister and one of golf's greatest enthusiasts of the period.

Islay did become a popular destination for the east coast golfers. In 1893 and 1894 some 25 per cent of the Islay Golf Club members came from the Edinburgh area, many of them returning year after year. Among them were W. Croal, the golf correspondent for *The Scotsman* and photographer William J.M. Rennie who provided 6 photographs of the course which appeared in yet another extensive article on Islay golf in the April 1898 issue of *Golf.*

When the golfing minister first joined the Islay Golf Club in 1893 he immediately made his presence felt by suggesting that Mount Zion was too difficult for

Rev. John Kerr of Dirleton

an opening hole and it would be better played as the 17th. His advice was immediately accepted. This was followed by his first article on golf on Islay in the *Golfing Annual* of 1894. The publicity gained can take much of the credit for the dramatic jump in membership from 64 in 1893 to 145 in 1895. This eleven page article covered the history of Islay, the links and the Golf Club, how to get there and a hole by hole description of the course with an explanation of the names of each one. An original copy of this *Golfing Annual* may be viewed in the Museum of Islay Life at Port Charlotte. Extracts from his writings are quoted elsewhere in this history.

Kerr wasn't a bad golfer either, having a handicap of 10 when he played in the Kildalton Cross in 1904, but lost by 5 and 4 in the first round to Iain Ramsay of Kildalton playing off 16. He met the same fate in 1909 but reached the next round in 1911 - thanks to the Rev. Branford scratching! He went no further but in spite of his lack of success he retained his enthusiasm for the Machrie maintaining that the course 'is one of the best, if not the best in the world'. This was quite a profound statement coming from one who golfed extensively throughout the country and the East coast in particular.

At this time, many comments and criticisms were made about the large number of golfing ministers in the community. Kerr's attitude was that 'the Kirk and gowf had a happy alliance in this quarter (i.e. East Lothian) as it should have everywhere'. Kerr was an avid collector of golfing memorabilia who, when he was declared bankrupt in 1913, perhaps may have been perceived as neglecting his pastoral duties in favour of sport. He died in 1921.

The End of an Era

As the success story of the Islay G.C. and the Machrie continued with Higginbotham still in command the club suffered a dramatic loss. At a Committee meeting in April 1906 the Secretary intimated the great loss at the death of their Captain, Higginbotham, at Machrie on 18th February. A whole page of the Minutes was devoted to an appreciation of his efforts on behalf of the Golf Club. Some of the comments were:

'He actively exerted himself to improve the course and promote the success of the club, his genial disposition and generous hospitality attracted numerous visitors, he practically made Machrie his home since first elected Captain, no man was more highly respected nor better known among golfing circles, his intimate knowledge of everything pertaining to golf enabled him to settle all disputes without difficulty, he encouraged golf by giving numerous prizes and finally, to the Islay Golf Club his loss is irreparable.'

Mr. Higginbotham had left the club in good shape with 180 members, a healthy bank balance of £240 and a course with a growing reputation throughout the country.

The President, the young Iain Ramsay of Kildalton, offered to provide a prize in memory of Mr. Higginbotham and suggested it should be called 'The Higginbotham Challenge Trophy', that magnificent silver club still much fought after today . The first winner was J. S. Mcdonald who beat J. Badenoch.

The problem of finding a suitable successor was solved by appointing Iain Ramsay, as Captain. He was also made an Honorary Life Member as were Peter Reid and John Bolland for their long service to the Golf Club. With the Captain (and landlord) now likely to take a greater interest in the affairs of the Club, it was decided to pay the £10 due for ten years' rental in arrears!

A High Hazard on the Islay Golf Links

On 16th May 1908, another poetic work appeared, devoted solely to golf on Islay. It was hand-written and signed 'T.F.G.' which suggests it was written once again by Dr. T. F. Gilmour who was still on the Committee and who was belatedly taking up the challenge quoted in the previous chapter.

'The Scotsman's Maiden'

A high hazard on the Islay Golf Links

Let others seek their loves by night
And rave about the joys they feel
I woo a maid in broad daylight
And meet her armed with clubs of steel.
Like Lady Fortune at her wheel
She smiles upon me grave and sweet
When, full of Hopes and Fears I kneel
And lay the round world at her feet!

Ah gracious lady! from the Tee
The ball goes like a shooting star!
The 'Maiden' has been good to me
And sent me 'over ' sure and far.
Anon, wherever others are,
I lie safe, after a good drive,
And barring those mishaps which mar
May well hole out in four or five.

> At Machrie Links on Laggan bay
> A lovely and sequestered spot
> We meet together, day by day.
> For rain or shine it matters not.
> The faithful tryst is ne'er forgot.
> She never fails, although now and then
> She treats me to the common lot
> By smiling more on other men!
>
> For whither 'tis to show her power,
> Or more caprice or evil hap
> She looms up hugely like a tower
> And takes the ball into her lap!
> Then must I woo her half an hour
> Kissing her every here and there
> Or ever I can part from her
> My wilful lady debonair!
>
> When I am fortunate with her
> My heart is eased of half its load,
> I have no fear of Manipur
> Glenegedale's a beaten road
> The Punch Bowl but an episode
> Ifrinn and Machrie feasible-
> And though Mount Zion's high - ecod
> My 'score' is quite presentable.
>
> T.F.G. 16.v.'08

Dr. Gilmour's poetry had improved over the years but not his golf as his handicap fluctuated between 26 and 30 during his spell on Committee (1892-1916).

Problems on the Course

In spite of all the praise lavished on the Machrie in the aftermath of the £100 golf tournament mounting criticism was being directed at greenkeeper John McMillan. In 1908 a letter from the President, Iain Ramsay complained about a fire on the links caused by burning of the bent (long grasses). The police were called in but they failed to discover the cause of the fire. The greenkeeper was also under fire, as several informal meetings were held to consider written complaints from members about the condition of the course. McMillan was instructed 'to be more particular in cutting greens and in general to get the course in better condition'.

As the popularity of golf spread, everywhere members were demanding better playing conditions. The majority of the Islay G.C. members were from the mainland so naturally they expected the course to be maintained to the same standard as the mainland courses. A letter from a group of members outlined the higher standards demanded:

1. Course to be mown to a reasonable width.
2. Modern double bottom tins to be provided to keep flags straight.
3. Bents to be eradicated on line of play.
4. Grass round several of the greens to be cut to allow run on to the green from a pitch.
5. Part of the field at Mt. Zion to be taken into the course and the sand at the right hand side to be turfed over.
6. The keeper of the green to be instructed to generally keep things in first class order.

The Committee duly made a public announcement that these items would be attended to in future. Six months later, the Secretary ordered 16 spring flags with tassles and 18 hole tins with double bottoms at a cost of £7.13s.8d. At the 1909 A.G.M. as the letters of complaints were being read out, the meeting was suddenly adjourned. When re-convened three weeks later the numbers present had more than doubled from 5 to 11! Not a good response from a membership of 158 but at least a precedent had been established of holding the A.G.M. in August to coincide with the Kildalton Cross week. The expected extensive discussion about the course did not materialise at the A.G.M.

The greenkeeper was not yet clear of criticism as one month later the President complained that McMillan could not be found when wanted and that there was difficulty in getting good caddies. He was instructed to be in attendance at the clubhouse from 10.00am to 10.30am and from noon to 1.00pm. There were some sympathetic ears on the Committee as he was then instructed to spend as much time as possible in 'rolling the greens and cutting the course'. He was further appeased in the next sentence which suggested a letter should be sent to Miss Mackay of Machrie Farm asking her to keep her cattle off the course and further that something should be done to prevent the cattle and horses of Glenegedale from wandering over the course! That was the end of the complaints about the greenkeeper.

Course conditions had obviously improved as greenkeepers' wages had increased by 25 per cent in the following year. With a surplus of £333.15s.8d. it was proposed at the next A.G.M. that a home should be built for McMillan but Mr. Ramsay refused permission. He was then sent off to the mainland on holiday with the blessings of the Committee and a present of three guineas to cover his expenses

Machry Bay and Golf Course

Mrs Lucy Ramsay

to visit Prestwick, Troon, Turnberry, Bogside, Ranfurly, and any others he chose, to see how putting greens were kept and to gain some knowledge of their methods of winter dressing. Confidence in the greenkeeper had been restored and an extensive winter programme of work on the course was subsequently instigated, including an agreement to proceed with picking daisies on the putting greens. After the completion of the winter programme McMillan and his assistant Archie Johnstone requested an increase in wages and were granted 2/- and 1/- per week giving respectively 22/- and 16/-. Two years later when war broke out, McMillan had an increasing membership to keep happy, including more and more ladies who were beginning to gain more recognition.

The Arrival of the Ladies

Although the notice of April 1891 advertising the formation of the Islay Golf Club indicated that the Committee had 'laid out a small Course for their lady friends', it did not warrant a mention in the Minutes. Recognition of the ladies (golf wise) was very slow to appear in the Islay Golf Club. The negative Victorian attitude to the participation of ladies in golf prevailed for some years after the opening of the course. This is not surprising considering the attitude adopted by the men of the Ramsay family. The late Freda Ramsay quoted that, 'while the men played golf, the ladies went horse riding along the Big Strand. The ladies were not allowed to play golf because the men thought it was almost indecent for ladies to play golf!' Others might have added that it was almost impossible due to their tight restrictive clothing and ankle length dresses. The R.& A. were not in favour either as recorded in a letter from an official:

> 'Constitutionally and professionally women are unfitted for golf. They will never last two rounds of a long course in a day. Nor can they hope to defy wind and weather. The first Ladies Golf Championship will be the last!'

This letter was sent in 1893 to the newly formed Ladies Golf Union which has just recently celebrated its Centenary!

The first lady mentioned in the club Minutes was Mrs. Lucy Ramsay when she opened the course. For the next 18 years the only ladies' names recorded were her daughter's and her own, not for golf, but as generous donors of prizes, generally silver or gold. For example, when Iain Ramsay became of age in 1899 his sister presented a silver quaich in an old oak case which was won by Ronald McArthur.

The absence of facilities for lady golfers was commented on by another well known golfing minister, the Rev. John G. MacNeill in 1900. In *The New Guide to Islay* he devotes seven pages to the Machrie Golf Links and makes a plea on behalf of the ladies:

'Is there not plenty of room on the attractive links of Machrie for a ladies' golf course? It is high time the lords of creation emerged from their selfish exclusiveness to show chivalrous devotion to their helpmeets whose influence so unmistakably tends to elevate and refine man's nature.'

The words fell on deaf ears. The first glimmer of hope for the ladies appeared at the 1909 A.G.M. when a special resolution resolved to form a small ladies' putting course. A contemporary tourist brochure suggests that 'a ladies course of seven holes has been formed close to the Club House'. In accordance with the general attitude to ladies' golf at this time the 'course' would probably have been seven long putting holes only. At the same time they were allowed the privilege of playing the course at a cost of 5/- per year, 2/6 per week or 1/- per day, approximately half the men's rates. Recognition at last. Although prior to this some lady visitors were allowed to play the course, this was their first opportunity to join the Golf Club. The first recorded lady member was Mrs. G. Feaveryear who paid her 5/- to join on 4th May 1910. She was joined by another 17 ladies in this first year of admission as members.

In sharp contrast was the consideration given to the ladies of the County Antrim G.C. in Ireland who were allowed to form their own club in 1891 as a branch of the men's club. Three years later they formed a completely separate ladies Golf Club with their own 18 hole course and clubhouse.

Further progress appeared to come in 1912 when it was agreed at the A.G.M. that the ladies needed a lavatory to be provided in an extension to the gents' clubhouse. The 13th year of the century proved unlucky for the 38 lady members when, having put the matter to the Superior, Mr. Ramsay, the Committee agreed with his view that 'further consideration of the matter be deferred until a more opportune occasion'. Before it could be pursued any further war broke out and the subject was shelved.

More changes at the 19th

At Whitsunday 1900 Iain Ramsay agreed, with Miss Jessie Mackay, a lease of Machrie Hotel and farm for 15 years at a rent of £230 p.a. for the first five and £250 thereafter. Her sister joined her in running the hotel and since they had been housekeepers at the Machrie and White Hart Hotels respectively, it was an ideal partnership.

Iain Ramsay, continuing his father's development policy for the Machrie, offered, as a condition of the lease, to carry out extensive internal improvements and to build a new wing with additional bedrooms and facilities. A gravitational water supply was also to be taken into the house and hot water supplied in the kitchens and bathrooms. The golfers' interests were safeguarded by other conditions of the lease which ensured that the Hotel must be kept open for golfers and others, and that they were to have free access to the links. The proprietor also reserved the right to convert an outhouse into a home for the greenkeeper or any other purpose in connection with the Islay Golf Club. Two loose boxes were also to be reserved for stabling horses.

The lease of the farm and hotel had been held by members of the same family since its inception. Freda Ramsay considered that it was during the Miss Mackay era that Machrie Hotel attained its very high reputation.

By 1913 the popularity of the Machrie Links had reached a peak. The club had more than 200 members, the ladies were belatedly getting more recognition which resulted in their numbers increasing, the greenkeeper was satisfying the members and Miss Mackay had made a success of the Machrie Hotel. The future looked good in all directions but events in Europe were about to change the outlook completely.

CHAPTER FOUR

THE GREAT WAR PERIOD

Effects of the War

In 1913 the Islay Golf Club was experiencing its most successful period since inception with a membership of 201. When War broke out in August 1914 there were 20 fewer members and the ladies numbered 26. By the end of the month the Prince of Wales had put out an appeal for the National Relief Fund, which resulted in the club agreeing to donate £50. It was actually sent to the Glasgow Herald Shilling Fund for a similar purpose. It didn't affect the end of year balance sheet which showed a healthy surplus of £450.18s.3d. In 1915 when the membership dropped to 87 gents and 4 ladies, income was down 70 per cent so the greenkeeping wages were cut by 50 per cent by paying off McMillan's assistant. Through good management the Club was able to stay in the black throughout the war years in spite of a drastic reduction in income.

    The Hon. Secretary at the outbreak of war was Malcolm McIntyre who was a partner with Iain Ramsay in the Port Ellen Distillery. When he got down to scratch in 1911 he succeeded Peter Reid as the Club's best local player and also took over as Secretary from Peter Reid when he stepped up to become Captain. He was back up to a 2 handicap in 1912 when he was runner up in the Higginbotham Challenge for the third time and then completed his hat trick of wins in 1914. Further success came his way in 1914 when he reached the final of the Kildalton Cross which he had won two years previously. His handicap was plus 2 as he faced up to the well known Edinburgh player J.S. Graham off scratch. Unfortunately, he lost by 3 and 2 but as the only plus man in the field his performance in competing with the best from the mainland must have given a welcome boost to other local players.

Having also taken on the Treasurer's post in 1914 he was awarded an honorarium of £5.5s. in recognition of his increased work load. It was reduced to £2.10s. in

Mr Osborne, manager of "Port Ellen Distillery" in the centre.

Malcolm MacIntyre

1915 as he had enlisted in the army but the following year he submitted his resignation in a letter sent from the front line. The Committee refused to accept it and promptly increased his honorarium back to the original sum. Regrettably that was the last mention of Malcolm McIntyre in the Minutes as he did not survive the War. Iain Ramsay did return with the rank of Captain but as an invalid. With all competitions now cancelled for the duration of the war, fate was about to deal another blow to the club.

Towards the end of Jessie Mackay's tenure, she and her sister retired to Port Ellen and they appointed Duncan C. McIntyre from the Argyll Hotel in Oban as manager. However, the popular proprietrix died in 1916 and the delay in finding a new owner resulted in the closure of the Hotel during the summer of 1917. The effect on the Golf Club was drastic as membership plummeted to a war time low of only 48 gents and 4 ladies. Over the years when funds were short the members had responded by taking out life membership which now cost £5.5s. One of those to respond thus was J. Logan Mackie, son of P.J. Mackie. He paid his £5.5s. in 1913 but sadly he was killed in action in Palestine in the last year of the war while serving with the Ayrshire Yeomanry.

There wasn't much action on the course during the war although a competition was held in 1918 in aid of the Red Cross. It attracted 46 competitors out of a total membership of 57 including the ladies. As usual the prizes were generous but the proceeds were only £8.3s.2d. The scoring wasn't improving over the years as shown by the results:

Gold Medal	presented by the Club	won by A.V. Prescott	89 - 4 = 85
Silver Cross	presented by Capt. Ramsay	won by J. A. Farquharson	91 - 5 = 86
Bronze Cross	presented by Robt. Macfarlane	won by I. L. King	104 -18 = 86
3 Golf Balls	presented by the Club	won by Lt. Alexander	93 - 6 = 87

The wooden spoon was won by Mr. O'Malley with a score of 122 net.

On the same day a mixed foursome competition was also held. As the first record of such a competition in the Minutes the scores are worth recording:

Miss Gallery and Mr. Forbes	97
Miss Abercrombie and Mr. I. L. King	102
Miss McLellas and Mr. Scott	116

Later in the year at the A.G.M., the Chairman J.S. Cameron expressed the members' satisfaction with the good order of the greens, the only drawback being the absence of ordinary members who were 'more interested in the state of their game than the state of the funds'. Only four were present!

Getting back to Normal

As Armistice day arrived things started to get back to normal. The Club trophies came back from the temporary care of D. Osborne, manager of Port Ellen Distillery and Mr. Allan of Lagavulin Distillery, to be put back on show in the Machrie Hotel. The trickle of returning golfers of 1918 turned into a flood in 1919 when membership was back to pre-war levels of 171 including 33 ladies. All major competitions were restarted as many top class golfers returned to Islay. In spite of a healthy financial statement it was decided to increase income. At the A.G.M. in 1919 the seven members present were equally divided on the proposal to again introduce an entrance fee of 10/6 but it was passed on the casting vote of the Chairman and Captain of the club, Dr. D.M. Farquharson, safely returned from the war. No casting vote was needed as it was agreed the gents' subs remain at 10/6, unchanged since 1892, but the ladies' subs went up from 5/- to 10/6. Weekly and daily tickets were substantially increased, the gents respectively from 5/- to 7/6 and 1/6 to 2/- and the ladies from 2/6 to 5/- and 1/- to 1/6. The ladies had some justification for feeling aggrieved as they took the brunt of the increases. They registered their objections the following year when only ten joined the club, but in spite of this, income increased by 72 per cent. The Islay Golf Club was now fully back to normal and on a sound financial footing.

CHAPTER FIVE

BETWEEN THE WARS

Prominent Golfers at Machrie

Many of the top class golfers of pre-war days returned to Islay after the war, to be joined by newcomers enticed over by the ongoing publicity. A 1923 brochure on the Machrie Links commented that, 'they are without doubt the finest links in Scotland. Indeed many golfers enthusiastic in their praise say there is no better natural course in the world'. The quality of the golfers was high, a trend which continued for two decades. For example, in 1920 the percentage of golfers with handicaps of three or less was 40 per cent and 50 per cent in the Kildalton Cross and the Mackie Quaich, respectively. In the latter, 50 per cent of those had a plus handicap.

Among the returning pre-war stars were P.D. Hendry and H.G. Hendry, E.D. Evans, R.A. Lambie and J.S. Graham. The Cross was the magnet which brought them back but there were no local low handicap players about to challenge them. Instead a new generation of low handicap golfers mostly from the West of Scotland took up the challenge, were successful and by their repeated visits consolidated Cross Week as the hub of Islay golf. The newcomers destined to make their mark in administration and on the course in the 1920s and 1930s included J. McBean, P.E. Soutter, Matt Armstrong and R.C. MacGregor. Their feats are recorded later in the chapter devoted to the Kildalton Challenge Cross but there was one notable other star who was a member of the club for several years without competing in the Cross.

This was Robert Scott Jnr. from the Glasgow Golf Club whose name first appeared as the winner of the Captain's prize in July 1921. In spite of a +5 handicap he won this bogey competition, 2 down with Eadie Taylor (1) second at 9 down! His scores of 76 and 78 were in uncharted waters as far as Islay amateur golf was

Presentation of Kildalton Cross in 1920's by Mrs. Iain Ramsay to winner. To rt. of the "Cross", Captain Iain Ramsay, Hon. Secretary Mr. Etoe and P. E. Soutter Snr. (seated) with D. C. McIntyre behind him (with hat).

concerned. It was unfortunate he didn't stay to compete in the Cross but his handicap was increased to + 7 just in case. Scott went on to reach the semi-final of the British Amateur Championship the following year and then was first amateur in the Open at Troon in 1923. These performances helped him to a place in the 1924 Walker Cup team when, partnered by the Hon. Michael Scott, they gained the team's only foursome point against Bobby Jones and his partner. He was also capped for Scotland from 1924 to 1928 inclusive.

Scott's low scoring had made a mockery of the scratch score at Machrie which still stood at 82 when in 1922 the Islay G.C. joined the newly formed Scottish Golf Union. The club proposed that the scratch score should be 78 but the S.G.U. thought it too high and a scratch score of 76 was finally agreed rather reluctantly by the Committee who countered the local objections by increasing all local handicaps by 4. There was no increase for mainland member John McBean (+1) who hadn't got beyond the third round in three attempts at the Cross. His perseverance paid off in 1922 when he beat D.L. Hutton in the final. Unfortunately the Treasurer's book from 1928 to 1938 is missing so we can't be sure how long some of these top players remained members unless they won a trophy or joined the Committee. McBean was still around as Captain in 1928-29. So also was P.E. Soutter who first joined the club in 1915. He was an outstanding golfer from Hamilton Golf Club, he was Islay's Captain from 1922 to 1924 and was very much the guiding light of the Club between the wars. The Soutter family almost monopolised the Cross especially in the 1930s but the monopoly was broken in 1933 by the arrival of R.C. MacGregor from the Western Golf Club (Gailes). He was destined to become Islay's most successful golfer as he won the Cross in 1933 and 1935 but his best was yet to come post-war. However, there were other interesting changes and events taking place in this period.

Sunday Golf

Breaking the Sabbath by playing golf was an emotional subject repeatedly debated in newspapers, golf journals and Clubs throughout the first half of this century and before. The Irish at Dublin Golf Club had an early solution. If you want to play golf on Sunday, enter by the back door 'in deference to his lordship's wishes', an option not possible on Islay- the clubhouse only had one door!

The early attitude to Sunday golf on Islay is clearly stated in an article in *Golf,* dated 27 August 1897, where reference was made to the prominent church dignitary, Principal Rainy, who had been playing golf at Machrie every week day:

'Of course in Islay Golf on Sunday must not be thought of let alone spoken about but there is in the minds of some who are of the Constitutional Party even a more heinous sin than Sunday Golf. The Principal, it may be remarked is better at Kirk politics than at Golf. One day while the Principal's party were debating the evils of Sunday Golf in the presence of a highly respected local lady they were shocked by her comment that she did not think it was so bad to be putting on the greens on the Lord's day as to be passing Declaratory Acts.'

Little did the lady know that she had just hit the first shot for Sunday golf on Islay, but it would take a long time before it materialised officially.

Sunday golf appears thereafter to have developed gradually at Machrie without official recognition by the club. The local ministers noticed the trend and sent a joint letter of complaint to the Committee in July 1924. At the A.G.M. after much discussion it was decided to take no action other than to agree that the employment of caddies on Sundays was prohibited. The Committee were spared the problems of Portrush Golf Club which, two years previously, was taken to court by the clergy to prevent Sunday golf.

Murdoch MacTaggart, Captain 1932-33 at presentation of Kildalton Cross to Roy MacGregor in 1933.

J. Wilson, Captain 1934-35 at presentation of Kildalton Cross to Roy C. MacGregor in 1935.

About this time a discreet method of getting a little Sunday practice was to go for a walk over the links with golf ball in the pocket and the obligatory walking stick with its handle of course in the form of a wooden putter or driver and sometimes an iron or mashie head. Appropriately, they were known as Sunday clubs.

The situation was still unchanged in 1948 when next discussed in Committee. It was confirmed that there was no objection to Sunday golf provided no club employees were asked to work. Full recognition came in 1955 with the issue of day tickets for Sunday visitors. No competitions were allowed as Bert Marshall the hotel proprietor found out when he wanted Sunday competitions introduced. The barriers started to come down in 1961 when Sunday play was allowed for the Machrie Salver (presented by Dr. Kenneth Cross) and in the Locals v Visitors match. The final obstacle was removed at an E.G.M. in 1966 when it was agreed that medals could be held on either Saturday or Sunday.

Lease negotiations

The period just after the war was one of uncertainty for the Machrie Hotel, the Golf Club and the Ramsay family. As mentioned previously, the death of Jessie Mackay and the closure of the hotel in 1917 were bad news for the Golf Club, struggling to encourage the return of the pre-war members. Although Jessie Mackay's lease of the Hotel and farm had expired in 1915, it was January 1920 before the lease was signed in the name of Duncan C. McIntyre who was to play an important part in the future success of the Golf Club. The lease was for 14 years, effective from Whitsunday 1917.

The Ramsay family experienced hard times after the war and had to put up for sale the entire 51,324 acres of the Kildalton and Oa Estates in several lots. The split up of the estate affected the Golf Club in that it would have two landlords for the course. It also affected Ronald McArthur who, as a great admirer of the Ramsay family was very upset at the break-up. According to the late Freda Ramsay he took his own life in 1921. His brother, 'the Artist', also died tragically after falling from a bridge parapet into the river. Inside the Kildalton Church, Ronald's gravestone can be seen, inscribed as the blacksmith of Port Ellen but with no reference to golf.

In these times of difficulty, Captain Iain Ramsay, a casualty of the War, in a final act of benevolence to the Islay Golf Club offered to sell them the course for £100, a sum equal to the legal fees for the Deed of Sale. This information was supplied by the late Freda Ramsay but strangely the subject did not appear in the Club Minutes. Perhaps it was just a verbal offer dismissed out of hand, certainly not for financial reasons as the Club's balance at December 1922 stood at £458.

Never on a Sunday – Machrie 1892 (National Museum of Scotland).

With hindsight it is difficult to see how this offer, if made officially, could be turned down even although it equated to 100 years of current rental which had been static since 1891. For comparison the Glasgow Golf Club were happy to pay £2,700 in 1927 to purchase their course at Gailes.

After the sale the Club officials must have soon regretted the missed opportunity when they found that the two new landlords for the course each had opposite views regarding the value of the land. Holes 2, 3 and 4 were on Kintra Farm land, now belonging to Mr. MacTaggart, a sympathetic landlord who was prepared to lease the land for a mere £2 p.a. for ten years on condition that his cattle could graze on the course. The remainder of the course on the Machrie ground was bought by a Mr. Hindle who was quite the opposite. Obviously intent on recovering his investment as quickly as possible, he soon indicated he wanted a rental of £30 p.a. for 7 years effective from Whitsunday 1924, the lease to run concurrently with that held by Mr. McIntyre for the hotel and farm.

As a result of the vastly increased rental, the Club was soon operating at a loss and had to resort to a bank overdraft as an alternative to cashing in their War Loan Securities. Inevitably subscriptions were increased from 10/6 to 15/- for 1927

John MacMillan, Greenkeeper

Final of Kildalton Cross, 1935.

when they only broke even thanks to donations from Vice-President Dr. Chadborn, Dr. Murray and Mr. and Mrs. D.C. McIntyre.

When both leases expired in 1931 new terms were soon agreed. The Kintra rental was unchanged at £2 p.a. for 5 years but with an additional lump sum payment of £40 to Mr. MacTaggart. This was equivalent to an average annual rent of £10 which was a considerable increase for 3 holes. Fortunately there was no such increase for the Machrie ground now owned by Mr. D.C. McIntyre who had also taken over ownership of the hotel. Having now been manager or proprietor of the hotel for 17 years he appreciated the problems of the golf club and the hotel's dependence on it for success. His offer of an unchanged rental of £30 p.a. for ten years was quickly accepted but with the term reduced to 5 years.

The hotel owner, Duncan McIntyre, had been greens convener since 1931. As the time for renewed lease negotiations by the Club for McIntyre's part of the course approached in 1936, he was congratulated on the condition of the greens. The Captain, William Walker of Foreland, Islay, was prominent in the negotiations as he tried to acquire the Machrie lease for 21 years with breaks at 7 and 14 years and no change in rental. He had to settle for a 5 year lease and the same rental. The Kintra rental was increased to £3 for the same period. Mr. Walker had done well. He presented the aptly named 'Foreland' Trophy which was first competed for in August 1938. The first winner was his son-in-law, Stanley P. Morrison, founder of the whisky broking firm of the same name and father of Tim and Brian Morrison.

Thanks to the co-operation of Messrs. MacTaggart and McIntyre, the lease negotiations for this period, 1936-1941, had been successfully completed on reasonable terms to the Golf Club without too much hassle, but this was only the calm before the storm.

The Greenkeepers

In 1918 the members had expressed their satisfaction with the good order of the greens. Greenkeeper John McMillan was doing well and for his efforts he was awarded a War bonus of £5. Two years later his endeavours gained him another £5 bonus and a wage increase to £2 per week. His assistant was Willie White earning 30/- per week. For whatever reason, the increases were unsatisfactory as by the end of that same year their wages had increased to £3 and £2 respectively. In 1922 specialist advice was sought from Carter & Co., seed merchants which resulted in extra treatment to the greens.

Safety at work and working conditions were receiving much attention at this time throughout the country and the Workers Compensation Act was introduced. As a result, special accident insurance was taken out to cover the greenkeepers whose job was becoming more sophisticated due to the increased mechanisation and the general demand for improvement in the condition of courses. The R.&A. organised an appeal for funds to help with scientific research and the S.G.U. issued a similar appeal to which the Islay Golf Club sent £2.2s.

As McMillan neared the end of his career at Machrie, the Committee agreed to 'erect a new workshop for the professional and to convert the present shop to a caddy shelter'. He indicated early in 1933 that he would be retiring at the end of the season and a subscription list was opened. This raised the grand sum of £72.12s. which the Committee increased to £100 in recognition of his 40 years service. His natural replacement was his assistant, Willie White, at a weekly wage of £2.10s. Malcolm White was chosen from 15 applicants as the assistant greenkeeper at a wage of £1.10s.

When war broke out in 1939 the Committee reacted by immediately cutting the greenkeepers' wages, Willie from £2.10s to £2, Malcolm from £2 to £1.15s. and Donald Orr from £1.10s to £1. A big struggle lay ahead for the greenkeepers and the Golf Club.

Western Isles Open Championship

Notice of another great professional tournament for the Western Isles appeared in *The Glasgow Herald* of 11th December 1934. The news surprisingly emanated from London at a 'Ceilidh of the Western Isles'. Two tournaments were planned for the following summer, the Amateur Championship of the Western Isles and the Western Highlands and Islands Open. It was intended to change the venue each year but at this stage the first one was still undecided. No doubt, with tales still being told of the success of the Islay Tournament of 1901, it was a near certainty that Islay would be chosen for the first competition.

The idea was initiated by the Western Highlands and Islands Joint Council to encourage tourism through the golfing potential of the area. It became a reality through the generosity of the chairman of David MacBrayne Ltd., Sir Alfred Read, who provided the total prize money and trophies.

When the details were finally agreed, only one tournament was held incorporating both amateurs and professionals. Surprisingly the Islay G.C. do not seem to have been involved as it didn't appear in the Minutes. However, D.C. McIntyre as greens convener and hotel and course owner would know he was in for a hectic week.

With no Open Champions present this time, the quality of the field was not quite up to 1901 standards. The most prominent English professional was Archie Compston (Coombe Hill) who had been runner up to Jim Barnes (U.S.A.) in Prestwick's last Open in 1925 and third three years later behind Gene Saracen and

John MacMillan with Willie White

the winner for the third time Walter Hagen (U.S.A.). Ireland was represented by their two leading pros, P.J. Mahon (Royal Dublin) and W. Nolan (Portmarnock). The top Scottish competitors were Jimmy McDowall (Turnberry), the newly crowned Scottish Professional Stroke Play Champion, and Mark Seymour (Crow Wood). The furthest travelled pro was Angel de la Torre (Madrid), a prolific winner of the Spanish Open Championship. The leading amateurs playing were Hector Thomson (Williamwood) and R.S. Walker (Aberdeen University) who were joined by the Islay G.C. contingent of Colin and Angus White, Roy C. MacGregor and Stanley P. Morrison entered from Troon. The least known professional would be Islay's Willie White.

It was not for lack of inducement that many of the leading pros were absent. Total prize money was £500 which bore comparison with the £750 for the Open at Muirfield two weeks later. Most of the professionals competing at Machrie would receive some prize money, a reward for the English pros 'for their great daring in venturing so far from the beaten track and taking on a course where the old fashioned blind hole of the pre-war era still reigns supreme'. With the air service to the Western Islands in its infancy one of the English golfers caused quite a stir. After an overnight sleeper train journey from London he 'dropped down on the course from Renfrew'. Another well known English pro strode on to the pier at Port

Ellen, 'shouting for a taxi, apparently thinking he was still down the Strand. In the end he had to caddy his own clubs and bag through the rain'.

'Scrutator', sports writer in the *Glasgow Evening News* sets the scene as the far travelled pros prepared for battle, hoping to collect one of the first two prizes of 150 and 100 guineas:

'It is still raining like Billy-o and the English golfers gathered here for the Western Isles Golf Championship are waxing facetious about the rigours of the Scottish summer. So far Islay, clad in sombre garments of mist, is not giving itself any meteorological pat on the back. Albeit there is another brand of Islay Mist in the hotel which offers solace and forgetfulness to those who have sinned and suffered at Mount Zion or any of the other holes on the very sporting Islay Club course.

There is also cream which falls out of the jug like a divot, home made scones, home made preserves, all of them compensating clauses for the shrewishness of the weather, but the man who gave a Sassenach scribe soor dook for cream did not do Auld Scotland a good turn.

There are many quaint little touches about this Western Isles Championship which renders it noteworthy. Sleeping three in a room o'nights we have so many candles burning it looks like a wake, while a further rural note was the spectacle of the starter, Mr. Duncan Martin of steel shaft fame, shooing the ducks away from the first tee in order to let the Championship proceed.'

The weather was more suited to the ducks than the golfers on Tuesday, 11th June 1935 as the players experienced rain, mist, and gale force winds throughout the day. In spite of this young Pat Mahon played near perfect golf to lead the field by one shot after a first round of 72. He got a rare 4 at Mount Zion after bouncing from a wall on to the green. The favourite, Compston, playing in the worst of the weather when tents were blown down on the course, took 6 at the same hole and 7 at Willie's Fancy. In second place were W.J. Branch (Bristol) and T. Collinge(Swinton Park) along with McDowall, a stroke ahead of the amateur, Hector Thomson.

The best of the Islay golfers was Colin White on 80 followed by S.P. Morrison on 81 and R.C. MacGregor on 82. Mount Zion was prominent in the press reports and R.H. Ross (Lenzie) featured in one report by *Express* reporter, Bob Ferguson:

'How terrifying that third hole can be was exemplified in the case of R.H. Ross, a local amateur, who ran up a 10. Strangely enough most players find deep sand cavity behind the green their bogey. Ross was never behind. He took 8 to get up!'

He must have been shattered as he finished in 96.

The players woke on the second day in a different world. With a clear blue sky and perfect conditions it was expected that someone would break the course record of 70 held jointly by Willie White and P.E Soutter, the ex-Provost of Hamilton. Compston, first off the tee, was expected to do so but he only equalled it. McDowall after 34 to the turn beat the record by one shot, helped by a 2 at Punch Bowl and a 3 at Ifrinn. His 142 aggregate led the field by 2 shots from Collinge with Mahon and Branch on 145. Ryder Cup player Billy Davies showed his worth by also scoring 69. On the amateur front Thomson was on 149, a stroke ahead of Walker. The leading Islay golfer was Colin White on 157, two ahead of Morrison. The struggling Willie White scored 81 for the same total as MacGregor of 164. Hopes were high for more course records in the final 36 holes.

Glorious sunshine and a light wind set the stage for an exciting day of record breaking golf. The leader McDowall slipped back with a third round 75 as Collinge took the lead with a fine 70 for a 215 total where he was joined by Branch after a record equalling 69. Mahon shot 70 to be one behind, tying with Nolan after yet another 69. However, the real highlight of the morning was the new course record of 68 by Seymour but he was 7 behind and seemingly out of the running for a major prize. The low scoring continued as Willie Spark (Lanark) caused a shock with six 3's and three 4's to the turn which included a rare 3 at Mount Zion, but he couldn't keep it up.

The excitement mounted in the afternoon final round as Mahon went into the lead with 33 out while the others faltered. Davies was still within 2 strokes after 34 out but he couldn't touch Mahon's brilliant golf as he scored a record equalling 68 for a 283 total. It seemed all over until news spread that Seymour had followed his 32 to the turn with 3,3,3, all birdies. The spectators flocked out on the course to see his finish but there were no more fireworks. Having failed to get his 3 at Punch Bowl the chance of a tie had gone. Coming down the last needing a 3 for the 100 guineas 2nd prize, he overshot the green and then missed his 4 which would have shared 2nd place. However, he had the consolation of creating another course record of 67:

```
    3 3 4  5 3 3 4 4 3  = 32
    3 3 3  4 4 4  5 4 5 = 35   Total  67
           Results
```

P.J. Mahon (Royal Dublin)	70, 68	283
W.J. Branch (Hanbury)	69, 73	287
T. Collinge (Swinton Park)	70, 73	287
W. Nolan (Portmarnock)	69, 72	287
W.H. Davies (Wallasey)	71, 70	287
M. Seymour (Crow Wood)	68, 67	288

Mahon earned the 150 guineas for his first major success. Seymour received only £15 for his 6th place. However, someone had second thoughts on the lack of any recognition for his two course records. When he sat down for breakfast in the Machrie Hotel next morning recognition came in the form of a cheque for £10 lying on his plate.

Hector Thomson won the Amateur Championship with a score of 290. The leading Islay player was Stanley P. Morrison on 306 thanks to a final day total of 147. This earned him a silver salver for 4th amateur place but there was nothing for the next Islay player, Roy MacGregor on 316.

Pre-tournament doubts had been expressed about the wisdom of holding a professional tournament in such a remote location. These were countered by claims that the sponsors' aims had been achieved since the golfing public now knew where Islay was. After the tournament, its apparent success was queried due to the absence of the leading professionals especially Henry Cotton, winner of the Open the previous year. The timing of the tournament was also criticised because it was sandwiched between two successive tournaments in England and the inaugural Scottish Open at Gleneagles followed by the Open at Muirfield. There were few full time touring pros at this time so many couldn't be absent from their club for the six full days needed to participate at Islay.

The Western Highlands and Islands Joint Council didn't pursue the continuation of the Western Isles Open which speaks for itself. For the Machrie Links however, it certainly was a success due to the extensive and favourable press coverage.

Machrie Snippets

World Record on Machrie Links

Heard the one about the Englishman, the Irishman and the Scotsman on the golf course at Machrie? On 1st September 1913, Mr. R. J. Barton of Killiney G.C., Dublin playing with Mr. W. C. Achfield of Chevin, Derbyshire, hit a long approach shot towards the green of a blind hole, 354 yards long. Both were members of Islay G.C. and the Scotsman was John McNiven, a caddie in the game in front who was replacing the flag in the hole when the ball struck him on the head. The distance of the rebound was measured twice in the presence of three people at 42 yards 2 feet 10 inches and claimed as a British and world record rebound. It wasn't recorded whether the claim was made on behalf of the Irishman or the Scotsman! Twenty-seven days later it was demoted to a British record only, when a rebound of 75 yards was recorded off an African caddie. As late as 1973, when the *Golf Monthly* stopped publishing such information, the British record still stood.

Late on The Tee

On Monday 5th September 1932 two Glasgow golfers set out from Renfrew Aerodrome in a two-seater Gypsy Moth for a golfing holiday at the Machrie Hotel. At noon the pilot Mr. A.M. Dunlop and his golfing partner Mr. J.W. Robertson approached the landing field adjacent to the hotel in a 40 m.p.h. breeze. The pilot decided the field landing was impossible and attempted a cross wind landing on the Big Strand beach. The plane landed perfectly but was carried up the beach by a fierce gust. On reaching the high bents yet another gust threw the machine on to the golf course at the 6th hole (Achnamara) where it overturned completely and was wrecked. Golfers and holiday-makers rushed to the scene. They were astonished to find the two occupants, members of the Scottish Flying Club, crawling out unaided from beneath the wreckage with only slight injuries and pulling their clubs behind them.

The perfect ending to the story would have seen them starting the match at the 7th tee! However, that was not to be. They did the next best thing; after Mr. Robertson had his slight cut on his forehead dressed by Dr. Campbell McIntyre, son of the proprietor, the intrepid pair played their round of golf. Islanders and visitors cycled from all airts to see this first ever aeroplane crash on Islay. Nowadays the incident would be described as getting a flyer from the rough!

Aerial View of Machrie in 1930's

Hagen at Machrie

Walter Hagen was like a breath of fresh air to professional golf both in the U.S.A. and Britain in the 1920s and 30s. His flamboyant personality, his love of high living, and a reluctance to accept the lowly status in which the golfing establishment placed the professionals at this time, made him the favourite of the press and the public. His golf matched his personality as he won two U.S.A. Opens, four British Opens and five U.S.G.A. Championships.

He was advised by Tommy Armour that when in Scotland his golfing experience would not be complete until he had played golf at Machrie. He took his advice in 1937. Arriving at Central Station in Glasgow, he hailed a taxi and asked to be taken to the Machrie golf course. He was deposited on the pier, boarded the steamer and eventually reached the island and the golf course. The island grapevine soon spread the news of his arrival. When he arrived on the first tee the local club champion, complete with his 'tackety' boots was waiting to give him a game. The very excited local farmer, determined to impress, gave of his all, had a fresh air shot and fell over in the process. The round was duly completed but Hagen was not impressed. Back home in USA he challenged Armour and proceeded to describe the game and the course. Armour burst out laughing, "Oh laddie, you went to the wrong island you should have been on Islay, not Arran!"

However much the story has been enhanced over the years, one thing is certain, Hagen did play a round at Machrie, Arran. Current records show that he holds the course record of 59.

An Angel at Machrie

Alex Mackinnon as a boy watched some of the play in the Western Open at Machrie in 1935. One of the competitors was Angel de la Torre, a leading Spanish professional. Alex tells the story of how the small and slightly built Angel dropped his cigarette ash, presumably accidentally, into a cup of coffee belonging to Archie Compston. The 6ft.2in. English professional promptly picked up the slight Angel, put him over his knee and proceeded to spank him! At the least it might have given the Spaniard an excuse for his poor performance.

The Ladies - on The Fringe

The end of the 1914-18 war saw the ladies' membership soaring to pre-war levels. In the aftermath of the Suffragette movement, women got the vote and the ladies of Islay G.C. got their long awaited ladies' room. On 11th November 1920, the Committee decided to proceed with the extension to the clubhouse at a cost of £43.11s.9d. The contract was awarded on condition that work was finished by 31st December, just in time for the Ne'erday competition. It had taken 8 years to get approval but only 7 weeks to complete the work. The ladies had effectively paid for this work themselves due to the doubling of their subscription and green fees and the introduction of an entry fee of 10/6. A sharp reduction in the number of lady members resulted in the abandonment of their entry fee.

At this time, there were no official golf competitions for the ladies. Mrs. MacIntyre, wife of the proprietor, by way of encouragement, presented a prize for a mixed foursome competition in which the members of the Gartmain G.C. near Bowmore were asked to compete. There was no problem in avoiding a clash with the men's medal as the date fixed was 13th January!

The pattern for the ladies seemed to have been set with just the occasional mixed foursome competition and no obvious attempt to form a separate Ladies' Section, a situation which prevailed throughout the 1920s and 30s.

Stability and Continuity

For the Islay G.C. and the Machrie the period between the wars was a relatively stable one. Continuity of personnel was a prominent factor. D.C. McIntyre had been in charge of the hotel and the golf course for most of the time and the long-serving greenkeeper, John McMillan, had just retired to be replaced by Willie White, also with long experience of Machrie. Other members of the White family also played their part with Duncan as farm manager and sisters, Annie and Mary White, virtually running the hotel. His brother, Colin, who played in the Western Isles Open, also ran the sports shop in Port Ellen. The highlight of this period was undoubtedly the professional tournament but the most important factor was the continued success of the Kildalton Cross which was now established as an annual pilgrimage for many families. The encouragement given for greater participation by the ladies was also of significance. Stability had been achieved although lease negotiations always posed a threat for the future. However, that future was under threat as Hitler's armies were on the move across Europe.

CHAPTER SIX

WAR AND PEACE

Like most golf clubs in wartime, Islay struggled to make ends meet as the membership and income decreased quite rapidly. As if that wasn't enough, the problems were compounded by the death of their proprietor, lease renewals and two changes of proprietor, one of which resulted in a long-drawn-out period of acrimony.

War Breaks Out
When the last peace time A.G.M. was held on 1st August 1939, there was little cause for concern among the membership which included six members of the Soutter family. Subjects for discussion were normal. P.E. Soutter Snr. suggested a new tee was needed at the 5th and along with the Captain David Barbour and James Wilson he formed the sub-Committee to organise the Kildalton Cross week. At the suggestion of Joe Soutter, in the handicap calculation, a half hole should be rounded up to one hole. It was also agreed to reserve the 1st and 9th tees in the morning on Cross days. All was perfectly normal. Two weeks later P.E. Soutter Jnr. had won his second Cross and was given a scratch handicap. The tranquillity of Islay was shattered on 3rd September by the declaration of war.

The reaction by the Committee was immediate and typical: preserve the Club's resources by the only means possible, i.e. cut the wages of the three greenkeepers by varying amounts from 17 per cent to 33 per cent. It wasn't enough so they sold the Club's War Loan Securities. All competitions were cancelled in 1940 even although there were still 119 members listed, 28 down on the previous year. Visitors weren't coming so that income was halved which resulted in a balance of only

£7.7s.6d. at the end of the year. In October 1940 fate delivered it's first blow with the death of the proprietor, D.C. McIntyre which was recorded in the Minutes :

> 'He has been a true friend and a tower of strength all the time he was their proprietor and his loss was mourned by all.'

The arrival of the Royal Air Force in large numbers to the aerodrome at Glenegedale interrupted the downward trend in membership in 1941 when 35 of the 132 members came from the Services. The resultant improvement in income saw Willie White's wage increased back to it's pre-war level of £2.10s. and the final balance was three times the previous one. However, prospects were not too healthy with both lease renewals due in 1942 and a new landlord on the horizon for the Machrie ground and the hotel.

In spite of these facts, White's wage was increased in June 1942 to £3 per week in recognition of his additional work load as he now had only one part-time assistant. The R.A.F. Sports Officer asked for special terms for service personnel and was granted a 1s. reduction on a day ticket to 1s.6d. but in spite of their presence the inevitable downward slide in membership arrived with numbers reduced to 88 in total including only 14 from the Services. In 1943 the corresponding numbers had decreased to 65 and 5. Otherwise 1943 was a blank year in the Islay G.C. history as there were no Minutes of meetings or the A.G.M. recorded in the Minute book.

A New Regime

While the timing of the change in ownership after the death of D. C. McIntyre is less than clear, the new owner of the hotel, the farm and the relevant part of the course was Mr. Rosslyn Colam. The Minutes of the Golf Club restarted in January 1944 and included a letter from Colam offering to put sand on the greens and provide a horse and cart so long as the Club pay the man's wages. The Kintra rental had been agreed at £10, renewable annually, but there was no quick agreement with Mr. Colam on the Machrie lease. 1943 must have been a very trying year for the Club. In spite of the sale of 3 per cent Defence Bonds to the value of £150 to cover a bank overdraft, there was still a loss of £106.15s.9d. for the year. The remedy was drastic: the green fees were doubled but there was no increase in the subscriptions! Gent's weekly and day tickets now cost 20s. and 5s. with the ladies at 15s. and 4s. Concessions of 50 per cent were given on day tickets for men and women from the services. Negotiations with Mr. Colam for the new lease were unsuccessful and as tensions mounted the greens convener, Neil MacLeod, resigned in March 1944. Soon after, Willie White did likewise. In recognition of

Willie's 25 years of faithful service, a testimonial was raised which produced over £50. Colam was appointed greens convener but he didn't last. Six months later at the A.G.M. he was off the Committee. MacLeod and White were re-appointed with William Walker of Foreland back as Captain and Donald C. Orr, a solicitor from Hamilton, as Vice-Captain. Orr's appointment was significant as he had a leading part to play in the ongoing lease negotiations with Colam and his company, Islay Hotels Ltd. He outlined Colam's proposals for the new lease from 15th May 1945 should the Club wish to continue after that date. A classic end of lease situation was developing.

Colam had already given the Golf Club 'notice to remove' by the end of the lease. His terms were completely unacceptable and the members reacted at the A.G.M. by authorising a special sub-Committee led by Donald Orr to take immediate steps to make a 9 hole course on the Kintra ground if no agreement was reached. After several fruitless meetings, Orr wrote to Islay Hotels Ltd. with an ultimatum that unless satisfactory proposals were produced by 15th October the Club would take immediate steps to remove to Kintra. After no reply by December, the sub-Committee were authorised to arrange a lease and agree a rent with Iain Mactaggart, the landlord of Kintra, to instruct the greenkeeper to prepare to make the extra 6 greens and tees to give 9 holes at Kintra and to arrange for the removal of the clubhouse, tool shed, caddy shed and greenkeepers' workshop.

Within hours of the above decision, terms had been agreed for the lease of the necessary ground at Warrin, Kintra for 5 years at £10 p.a. plus a further £25 on signing the lease to cover damage to ground during course construction and for 'disturbance to the animals'. As a bonus Iain Mactaggart agreed to lease on similar terms sufficient ground extending towards Grianan to provide the full 18 holes. The Club had played their trump card but it failed to move Mr. Colam.

Going Public

As a stalemate situation developed the battle went public in the *Oban Times* of 3rd February 1945. A letter written by Colam was directed at the residents of Port Ellen to ensure they 'should appreciate the facts'. His prime fact was that the decision by a few members to build a new 9 hole course was made under the misapprehension that visitors to Islay would not be allowed to play the course after the end of the lease. It was of course not quite as simple as that. On 10th March Wm. Aitken's reply was published claiming that the Hotel's letter was misleading and he stated the true facts. Colam seems to have been ahead of the times in trying to establish an exclusive country club set up at Machrie. However, he had picked the wrong location, the wrong people and certainly the wrong time with the country still at war. Some extracts from Aitken's letter clarify the situation:

'Recently a bombshell was thrown into the Islay Golf Club. A warning out notice was sent and a list of conditions on which Machrie would take over the Club, not the course, was sent to the Club. These conditions included the taking over of the clubhouse, machinery, shelters and everything which goes to form a part of the course, without payment, an absolute veto on playing members by the manager of Islay Hotels Ltd. without assigning any reason. He desired to debar playing rights to anyone he thought fit even although this might include the cancelling of membership. No new members resident in Islay had to be allowed without his authority. Nothing was being conserved to the Golf Club, not even a personality or the ability to maintain itself as a Club.'

The letter continued in a reference to failed attempts by the Club for a compromise:-

'The members were told that what was wanted was a club for the hotel and complete and absolute control of it by them, and that the terms submitted could not be altered.'

After detailing the arrangements for the new course at Kintra and further unsuccessful attempts at compromise the letter concludes:-

'A course had to be preserved for the inhabitants of Islay as well as for visitors, and for all visitors to the island and the Committee would have been lacking in their duty in this, and a disgrace to Highland independence and love of those who love Islay and Islaymen had they accepted the terms proposed. The Committee are certain that no one could read the terms proposed without feeling that not only was the breakaway advisable but it was forced upon them without alternative.

Crisis Time

These were strong words necessitated by dire circumstances but they were successful in forcing Colam to be more reasonable. As Whitsunday 1945 approached the brinkmanship tactics of the Committee succeeded without the need to remove to Kintra. The war in Europe had ceased but not the war of words on Islay.

Another crisis developed at the A.G.M. on 25th August 1945 when a loss of £5.7s.11d. and only 77 members were reported for 1944. The Committee fell apart. The Captain, Wm. Walker declined to be re-elected for health reasons, as did D.C. Orr for business reasons and Wm. Aitken resigned after 10 years as Hon. Secretary because 'he could not see his way to continue any longer'. Their replacements were: Captain, David Barbour who had held the position in the early war years, Vice-Captain, Iain Mactaggart and Hon Secretary/Treasurer, J.R.H. Hall. Significantly, Colam was re-elected to the Committee. His revised lease conditions for the course were unanimously agreed including a refund to the Club of the Kintra rent and the greenkeepers' wages already paid for the year. The exact terms of the new lease were not quoted but the identity of the Islay G.C. had been preserved at

Machrie although Islay Hotels Ltd. had achieved their aim to take over responsibility for the upkeep of the course.

The Club increased subscriptions to £2.2s. for gents and £1 for ladies to help the financial situation and entrance fees were abolished in the hope of boosting the low membership of 46. However, the crisis was not yet over as in December the members were told by circular that there had been no progress in getting the agreement signed due to unexpected difficulties. These were financial ones whose resolution became urgent in April 1946 due to the imminent sale of the hotel and the Machrie part of the course by Islay Hotels Ltd. A 50 per cent reduction in the refund was agreed, Colam resigned from Committee and the Club and a huge sigh of relief was breathed by all. However, the problems still remained; namely, shortage of cash, decreasing membership and a course which wasn't at its best. There were only 34 members for 1946. The pre-war members had not been enticed back, possibly influenced by doubts about the future of the Club. The big imponderable question remained. What would the new landlord be like?

Struggle for Survival

The new owner was a company called Machrie Hotels Ltd. At the first official meeting with the Golf Club on 4th July 1946, its directors, Major A.D. Cameron and Hon. Geoffrey Cunliffe soon eased any concern by immediately stating that they wished to be on friendly terms with the Club, its members and the local people generally. They wanted the responsibility for course maintenance to return to the Club and offered to charge no rent until the Club was financially sound. As a bonus they offered to purchase any necessary greens machinery which would be hired to the Club with the option to purchase at a later date, any rental paid being offset against the purchase. The guardian angels had arrived! They also undertook to pay the Kintra rental and charge the Club an annual rental for the whole course. All that was asked for in return was co-operation from the Port Ellen hotels in assisting the Club to raise funds, the right to negotiate directly for either a long lease or the purchase of the Kintra ground and the right to go to a neutral arbitrator if the course wasn't maintained to their satisfaction. It seemed too good to be true.

As the Club struggled with its budgets the owners proposed that they waive tractor and mower hire charges and charge a nominal rental of 1s. for 3 years. They offered to trap and gas the multitude of rabbits on the course to help improve its condition. The foundations had been laid for the regeneration of the Golf Club but it couldn't succeed without new members. All absent members from 1939 were offered membership on payment of the next year's subscription and arrears were waived. The entrance fee was re-introduced for new members.

At the delayed A.G.M. on 24th October 1946, the Secretary reported on the year's circumstances and 'deplored the apathy of the members towards the interests of the Club and warned the meeting that, unless more active assistance is given, the chances of rehabilitating the Club were extremely poor'. Although he was able to report a current balance of £100, only 19 members had paid their subscriptions to date. Nevertheless, the arrangements for taking over the management of the course were approved and Willie White came back as greens convener with authorisation to engage a 'working greenkeeper' and an assistant. By the end of the year the outlook was still bleak as there were now only 34 members. In an attempt to get things back to normal, dates were fixed for the 1947 competitions, monthly medals were to be resumed and Willie's brother Colin was appointed professional and head greenkeeper. Dances and whist drives in the spring of 1947 produced £66 for Club funds and an appeal went out to several local businesses for financial help. As a last resort the green fees were also increased.

The financial burden of managing the course was proving too much because the expected return of members and visitors didn't materialise. Machrie Hotels Ltd. came to the rescue as guarantor for a £100 bank overdraft but as the situation deteriorated all 1947 competitions were cancelled. By July 1947, some members expressed the opinion that they should not have to rely on Machrie Hotels for survival, even although £500 was needed to cover wages and the purchase of new machinery to replace pre-war machines now beyond repair. The crisis deepened as the A.G.M. arrived with the course in very poor condition. The new machines promised by the proprietor had not arrived nor had the new members. Mr. Logan, the hotel manager, stated that some new equipment was on order for early delivery which should ensure the course would be in good order for 1948. This undoubtedly influenced the members in deciding to continue for another year. In an attempt to rally local interest the Committee was formed of local members only.

By October 1947, the proprietors had to bail out the Golf Club again with two deposits of £40 but the situation wasn't improving. There were only 31 paid up members by the end of the year. When Colin White then resigned, he was succeeded by a Mr. Menzies from Perth who arrived in February 1948 suggesting that he could have the course in good condition for the summer months 'if he had any working mowers'. There had been little mention of golf in the Minutes for the previous year but normality was resumed with discussions on cattle on the course, Sunday golf and the availability of golf balls. The latter were so scarce during and after the war that in some clubs the luck of the ballot decided who got a new Silver

King for the medal. On Islay with only 29 gents and 11 ladies distribution would be easy.

Dates were fixed for the competitions but there would be no medals until the membership increased. Before that could happen Machrie Hotels Ltd. decided to get out. The generous contributions and co-operation of Messrs. Cameron and Cunliffe had saved the Islay G.C. from extinction but they were now back in the 1943 situation of losing a good proprietor and wondering what the future held. Still in a poor financial state, thoughts of survival must have re-surfaced.

Peace

The Blackpool Highlander

The hotel, farm and course were bought by Bert Marshall from Blackpool. When he first met the Committee in April 1948 the Club's serious financial position had not been resolved. Marshall, yet another generous proprietor, immediately offered to help the Club as far as he was able. He paid the greenkeeper's wages for the rest of the year and continued payment into the next year. The contrast between the old and new proprietors was considerable. The Major and the Hon. Geoffrey had been replaced by a down-to-earth genuine character who reputedly arrived from Blackpool after a substantial win on the pools. He was renowned for his standard dress mode on his 20 stone figure - bare arms, open neck shirt, kilt and green wellies. The latter were a necessity as the outbuildings were still in use as a working farm.

At the 1948 A.G.M. the Hon. Treasurer, Mr. Corse, suggested that the Golf Club should either be wound up or a new financial agreement reached with Mr. Marshall to ensure the Club remained in existence. It was agreed to allocate all green fees and subscriptions to the upkeep of the course, to abandon the entrance fee and to form a juvenile section. In addition fortnightly tickets were reduced from £2 to £1.10s. for gents and from £1.10s. to £1 for ladies. The generous Bert conceded that any surplus at the end of this financial year need not be passed on to him.

The Turning Point

The struggle for survival continued but the measures taken only produced a marginal membership increase to around 40 for 1948 and 1949 so finance was still in short supply. There were, however, some good signs. The Soutter family re-appeared and brothers Alex and Dugie Mackinnon arrived on Committee. Whist drives, concerts and dances were organised by the locals and the £100 profit reported from these events at the 1949 A.G.M. was the turning point for the Club finances, aided by the continuing help from Bert Marshall. He offered to pay one of the two overdue payments of £25 for the Kintra rental, provided the Club pay the other. He also asked for permission to fence off the greens to allow him to graze his cattle on the course. When the greenkeeper Menzies was sent packing, only C. McMillan was left working on the course which was again overrun by rabbits. A local rule was introduced allowing the ball to be lifted and placed without penalty when a rabbit scrape interfered with the line of the ball - on the greens!

To gain publicity, the Kildalton Cross was put on display in Rowan's Sports Outfitters shop in Glasgow and thoughts were given to asking Sam McKinlay of *The Glasgow Herald* to pay a visit and write an article about the course. Second thoughts prevailed as it was realised that Sam's comments might be counter productive due to the state of the course. Having heard a story that in the 1950s the British Walker Cup team had practised at Machrie, the author wrote to him for confirmation. His reply was very blunt. The team had never visited the course and he doubted if any of them had ever heard of it. Obviously he had forgotten about his fellow Walker Cup player, R.C. MacGregor and his association with the Islay G.C. He did, however, admit to having visited Machrie on one occasion while on holiday at Port Ellen. He took his wife into the hotel for a coffee but found nobody and no coffee. Having struggled through the mud around the farmyard and stepped warily around the cow patches on the way to the first tee he turned around and headed back to Port Ellen. He was not impressed.

Alex Mackinnon

When he was 11 years old Alex remembers queuing at the gate on to the course waiting to be chosen as a caddie by the professional, Willie White. Normally he was given the same bag to carry each year so that Alex caddied for 4 years for J.C. Denholm of the Denholm Shipping Line. He was encouraged to take up golf by his client who at the end of each holiday presented him with some items of golf equipment for his own use. The nearest suitable field or garden in Port Ellen then became Alex's practice course before he eventually got a job in the Post Office.

His parents would forbid him going out to the course but it didn't stop him. In the evening he would slip his clubs on to an army lorry knowing it was heading for Machrie in the morning when he slipped out and had his round regardless of the consequences. On Islay in the 1930's an artisan golfer was an unknown species. When Alex joined the Golf Club in 1937 he reckoned he was probably their first ever artisan golfer. By 1939 he was a golf addict.

Islay G.C. have much to be grateful for in Alex's enthusiasm when he became Hon. Secretary and Treasurer. He reckons 1947 was the crunch year when the

Club almost failed. There was no money to pay a greenkeeper so the course deteriorated rapidly and it was only through the dedication of the local members that both course and Club were saved. Alex, in desperation delegated two local members to maintain each green. John MacIntyre Snr. who was manager of the Machrie Farm, also contributed by cutting the fairways using Bert Marshall's machinery.

The Resurrection

It was 1950 before the crisis was completely over, thanks almost solely to the local effort. On the course, a local gamekeeper, Alex McNeil, worked hard on a contract basis as greenkeeper from May to September only. As part of his agreement he was allowed to trap rabbits on the course, sell them and keep the proceeds. With food rationing still in force there was a ready market for them. He had to take payment by instalments as the committee set about raising funds. A plea to Bruichladdich Distillery for a donation of whisky for prizes in a raffle brought a refusal because they did not believe in free drinks. They sent a generous £100 donation instead! Other members and the Islay business community came to the rescue with donations for the raffle which eventually produced £2000. This along with the proceeds from numerous dances and ceilidhi put the Club on a sound financial footing. Alex Mackinnon and the local Committee helped to complete the resurrection by encouraging new local members which resulted in the membership doubling to 102 of whom half were local.

At the A.G.M., the Captain, Dr.D. Riddell Campbell, stated that the previous Easter the course was in very bad order indeed and he had been doubtful whether it could be saved. Great credit was given to Alex McNeil for the transformation of the course, to Alex Mackinnon for the transformation of the Club's position, to Willie White for his fund-raising and to Bert Marshall for his co-operation.

The large local involvement was recognised when the A.G.M. was changed from afternoon to evening and some medals were arranged for Monday evenings. The tide had turned for the Club. All that was needed now to boost moral further and to publicise the Club and the Machrie was a good performance on the wider golf scene. It came quickly from pre-war member Roy C. MacGregor who rejoined the Club in 1950.

Roy C. MacGregor

Roy hit the headlines in 1949 when, playing for Ayrshire against Glasgow in an inter county match at Ralston G.C., he scored 40 for 12 holes, 7 under par. This was quite sensational for this era. His putting streak of 11 putts for the 12 holes

Roy C. MacGregor, Captain 1954-55

included 9 single putts and two holed pitches. It earned him a mention in the 'Curious Scoring' records in the *Golfers Handbook,* alongside the famous Walter Hagen who had an 'incredible achievement of seven putts for nine consecutive holes'.

When Roy, a double winner of the Kildalton Cross in the 1930s, returned to Machrie in 1950 he had a scratch handicap at Western Gailes G.C. He made an immediate impact by beating Dugie Mackinnon 7 and 6 to win the Kildalton Cross. He also won the Mixed Foursomes with Mrs. A.D. Campbell and was runner up in the Peking Cup. He repeated his win in the Cross the next year against the same opponent. 1951 also saw the first of his four successive appearances for Scotland in the Home Internationals. His performances earned him a place in the Walker Cup in 1953 at Merion, Massachussetts. It was no success story for Roy as he lost both singles and foursomes when the U.S.A. won 9-3. He was Vice-Captain of Islay G.C. at the time and because of his selection he postponed his election as Captain until 1954. He thus became the only Captain of Islay G.C., to have played in the Walker Cup. Thereafter, business pressures restrictd his competitive appearances otherwise his list of honours could have been much greater.

At the A.G.M. he told the members that 'the course was as near perfect as he had ever seen it'. Expenditure was approved to repair the run down shelters on the course and, as an extra, strands of wire were added to keep out the sheep! There was no money available to purchase new timbers for widening bridges at Gara Tota and Texa to accommodate the latest innovation for golfers, the caddy car.

Cash Shortages Again

Cash shortage continued into 1955. Bert Marshall came to the rescue again when it was revealed that the Club only owned one 16" mower and a spiked roller. The remaining equipment consisting of a triple gang mower 3 mowers and 6 rollers all belonged to Bert who promptly presented all the equipment to the Golf Club on condition that they were used in close co-operation with himself. For good measure he also donated £30. At the A.G.M. Bert Marshall was elected Honorary President in recognition of his vast contribution to the Golf Club. Sadly, the death of Willie White was also intimated thus ending 35 years of devotion to the Golf Club as greenkeeper, professional, greens convener and Captain (1952-53).

The Ladies' Involvement

In the midst of the deep depression which hit the Golf Club after the war one lady came to the fore, not for her golf, but as the new Hon. Secretary. Mrs. Earl

Kildalton Cross finalists. Roy C. MacGregor (l.) beat Dugie Mackinnon in both 1950 and 1951.

Walker Cup Team of 1953. R.C. MacGregor in centre of back row.

(Peggy McCallum) was appointed in 1947 to succeed the Rev.D. Cameron who was leaving the island. She was a keen golfer with a handicap of 24 and it says a lot for her courage that she was prepared to accept this unenviable position in times of crisis. Two years later with the Club still in difficulties she resigned and in came Alex Mackinnon to start his rescue attempt. Her presence helped to focus attention to the contribution that the ladies could make, given the chance.

In July 1951 a ladies bogey competition was 'offered as an experiment'. It failed miserably as only 3 turned up but there were promises of more competitors for the next year! Although absent from the course the ladies were prominent in organising and helping to raise cash at the many functions throughout these years.

The uncertainties about the future of the Islay G.C. in the immediate post-war period had been overcome thanks mainly to the supreme efforts of the local members, coupled with the financial assistance and co-operation of Bert Marshall, which ensured that peace reigned once more at Machrie. As the course improved, the mainland golfers returned and the presence of a Walker Cup player undoubtedly helped to advertise the fine golf to be found at Machrie Links. The future looked brighter than for many years.

CHAPTER SEVEN.

A RUN UP TO THE CENTENARY

Although the crisis of the post-war period had passed, the golf club continued to experience difficulties, both financial and on the course, during the decades of the 1950s and 1960s. They were overcome through the help and dedication of the local members. A major setback was the theft of the principal club trophies. The years before the Centenary saw three changes of proprietor including the Morrison era which saw big improvements to the course and hotel complex. This was accompanied by increasing membership of the Islay Golf Club and more recognition being given to the ladies and the need to encourage the juniors.

On The Course

Although Roy MacGregor praised the near perfect condition of the course in 1954, it was no easy job to maintain this situation through the 1950s and 1960s. The age long problems were still present, cattle on the course, lack of experienced greenkeepers, old equipment and a shortage of funds.

The equipment problem was eased by the purchase of an Auto Certes greens mower in 1957 for £85 to be followed by the anonymous donation of another. After advertising in two shop windows in Port Ellen for a greenkeeper, Colin White got the job from April 1958 on a self employed basis at £7.10s. per week. The cows still roamed free over the course as the Committee agreed to erect fences to keep them off the greens in the winter. The following June the fences were still up as the cattle were still grazing and the fairways couldn't be cut due to the unavailability of the farm tractor. It was too busy making hay! At end of the year Mr. Marshall compromised by offering a tractor, provided the golf club could supply a driver.

The fencing was causing problems as the members asked for sacking to be put over the top barbed wire strands. Later, those taking the low road through the fence asked for the bottom strand to be replaced by a smooth one. Eventually stiles replaced the sacking. The greenkeeper's task wasn't easy. By the spring of 1959 the cows had caused irreparable damage to the first tee and the greens as they pushed their way through the fencing. In the summer of the following year, the farm tractor was still ploughing so gang rollers and tractor were borrowed from the airport. Alex MacNeil was the greens convener at this difficult time, but he was having some success as he was congratulated at the 1961 A.G.M. for the condition of the course. Two months later he had the Committee on parade helping to spread on the greens, peat dust which had been supplied by Lagavulin Distillery. He was rewarded for his efforts in 1962 when he was elected Captain.

The constant battle on the course continued throughout the 1960s. Casual inexperienced workers were often employed, so responsibility for maintenance of the mowers fell to John MacIntyre Snr., the Machrie Farm manager. He was also out regularly cutting the fairways as was Alex Brown who took over as greens convener after the death of Alex MacNeil in 1968. The efforts of these three volunteers ensured over many years that, in spite of the difficulties, the comments on the course were generally favourable at the A.G.M. A further step forward came with the decision to install electric fencing to the greens but due to the cash shortage only a few greens could be done at a time.

One of Alex Brown's early jobs was to cut three new holes at Glenegedale. The need arose due to the uncertainty of the year to year lease of the Kintra ground and the refusal of the owner to grant a longer one. At the A.G.M. in 1969 Alex was granted £25 for his hard work. Further doubts arose the next year when the course and hotel once again changed hands. The new owners, Thomas M. Lang, Alexander M. Gray and Iain Gray stated they wished to retain the Kintra ground for the future and also offered financial assistance to retain the greenkeeper for as long as possible at the end of the season. The future looked secure so more electric fences were bought. When Mr. MacTaggart confirmed he had no alternative plans for his ground at Kintra the maintenance of the new holes at Glenegedale was abandoned in 1971. However it was still proving impossible to find an experienced greenkeeper.

The Duncan MacCalman Era

Golf came to Duncan MacCalman late in life after a highly successful athletics career which began with a win at Powderhall, Edinburgh in 1926, aged 18. His success in winning the Argyllshire Trophy for the best all round athlete in 1929,

1930 and 1933 and the Oban Games Athletics Championship in 1931 brought him an invitation from the Duke of Argyll to visit Inveraray Castle to select a gift. It was typical of Duncan that he couldn't find the time to go as he preferred to concentrate on his own interests. When his athletic career was over, he returned home to Islay to set up in business as a haulage contractor. A normal day for this workaholic consisted of unloading sand, grain or coal from puffers at the pier on to his two lorries all by hand from dawn to 6 o'clock, often followed by 18 holes at Machrie.

Another love of Duncan's was studying and reading Gaelic which took him to the Mod where on several occasions he just missed the coveted gold medal. Fifty years of dedication to the Gaelic language and the Mod earned him a surprise presentation of a decanter during the 1981 Mod.

When he was first elected to Committee in 1955 he was a natural for entertainment convener and he was a regular and popular singer at the many Ceilidhi held to raise funds for the club. His duties on Committee didn't affect his golf as he won the Argyllshire Championship in 1955. A year later, now greens convener, he also won the Kildalton Cross which resulted in a handicap reduction to 2. At the annual dinner of 1957 the Captain, Melville Lang, stated that he had seen no one hit a ball further than Duncan MacCalman. When he stepped down from Committee in 1960 he had achieved his lowest handicap of one and was one of Islay's leading players of this period.

With the news that the 1974 Argyll County Championship was to be played at Machrie, a big push began to ensure the course would be at its best. Large quantities of course sand and fertiliser were bought as well as a new mower but the problem of finding a suitable greenkeeper still remained. It was solved in June 1972 when retired member Duncan MacCalman offered his services as greenkeeper. Since, at the age of 65, he couldn't see himself being idle, he saw this as the opportunity for a new challenge in life! The problems and pitfalls were known to him as he set about the job with his natural gusto, both on a part-time and full-time basis.

The condition of the course was always an ongoing problem but support was once again at hand. After complaints from visitors, the Committee decided that 'daisies which had developed to the disadvantage of players be brought under control' but only with the proprietors' approval in case the daisy killer affected the cattle. They in turn still sought pastures new resulting in more damage to the greens. The repair work was too much for the greenkeeper so Alastair Ross, manager of Bowmore Distillery and A. MacTaggart of Port Ellen Distillery supplied the labour to complete the fencing. Mr. Gray, one of the proprietors, contributed

Duncan MacCalman, Winner of Kildalton Cross in 1956.

by removing his cattle from the course by the end of April 1973. Lack of finance was still a problem. Terms couldn't be agreed for the tractor overhaul so Alastair Ross obliged again.

The members gave their support too as Mr.T. Epps donated £50 for the purchase of flagsticks and Bob Grant made and erected 15 new direction posts. John Callow who was to be Captain in two years time gave £20 for a new glass fronted notice-board. The biggest contribution came from the Distillers Co. who donated a surplus site hut for use as a new clubhouse. The contract for its erection was given to A. McDougall of Bowmore at a cost of £570.

Proposals were put to the A.G.M. in 1973 by A. Gray and J. Callow for the elimination of the blind holes on the course. Similar attempts had been made in previous years but once again the traditionalists won the day when the only agreed change was to re-route the 14th fairway to give a clear view of the green. Duncan MacCalman would have been happy with that decision but not necessarily with the one which decreed that 'the greenkeeping staff be instructed in course maintenance, especially during Cross week'.

Three months later the Club lost one of their most faithful servants with the death of Manning Ayres, Treasurer for the previous 17 years. Vice-Captain Bill Sime, expressing his regret, stated that, 'had Manning's golf matched his enthusiasm he would have been a world champion. He was a wonderful member who will be missed for many years to come'. Manning was succeeded by Douglas Keith.

MacCalman worked two days per week over the 1973-74 winter before being asked to go full-time in July to get the course at its best for Cross week. He did not believe in setting up an easy course. This may have had some bearing on the decision to appoint a Sub-Committee to fix the pin positions for that week. At the A.G.M. Dugie Mackinnon tried unsuccessfully to get the fairways widened. A few feathers must have been ruffled by the greenkeeper as 10 days later his resignation was reluctantly accepted to be followed quickly by reinstatement after a letter of apology from the Committee. Duncan MacCalman was criticised by some players because more often than not he set very difficult pin positions in important competitions. True to his beliefs, when challenged, his reply would be, "If I can do it so can they."

Club Championship

It was 1964 before the decision was made to have a Club Championship. Not surprisingly, I. McCuaig, who won the Kildalton Cross three years previously, was the first winner. Derek Gray took command in the 70s and 80s when he achieved an impressive five wins. His feat was equalled by Iain Middleton in

1994 but his chance of a record fifth successive win the following year was lost when John Edgar gained his third Championship. It should be interesting to see who will be the first to become Club Champion for the sixth time.

Theft at Machrie

In May 1968 the club was faced with the major incident of the theft of its main trophies. On 3rd May, an emergency Committee meeting was held to discuss the theft of the Club's five principal trophies from the Machrie Hotel the previous night. Those stolen were the silver Kildalton Cross, the Mackie Quaich, the Foreland Trophy, the Marshall Trophy and the Mrs. McIntyre Cup. The immediate reaction to offer a reward was not advised by the police. At the A.G.M. in August when the new Captain, J.B. Soutter, took over from Dugie Mackinnon, no progress had been made in finding the trophies or the culprits. The replacement of the Kildalton Cross posed a problem because, apart from the as yet undetermined cost, there was no mould available for a new casting. Since the police were still hopeful of recovery, it was decided to take no action before the next A.G.M. The first bit of good news came with the offer from Bert Marshall to donate a new Marshall Trophy plus replicas.

In spite of efforts by some of the members to loosen the tongues of some likely suspects by plying them with several generous drams of Bowmore and Lagavulin whisky, neither they nor the police could report any progress by the A.G.M. of 1969. Joe Soutter stated that Mrs. Ramsay had agreed to allow a mould to be taken from the original Kildalton Cross. The purchase of a new 'Cross' was approved, if the cost was reasonable, and the Committee were left to decide on the need to impose a levy on the members. Sponsors were to be approached for replacement of the other trophies. Seven days later, Hon. Secretary Ralph Middleton informed the Committee that Mrs. Paterson of the Marine Hotel in Troon had very generously offered to donate a new Kildalton Cross to the Islay G.C. A member of the Soutter family had once again made a major contribution to the Islay G.C. as Mrs. Paterson was a sister of Joe Soutter.

The situation improved in June 1970 when, using some of the insurance money, a new Mrs. McIntyre Trophy was purchased for £300. Of more importance was the completion of the new 'Cross' at a cost of £2000. The first task of the Captain, John MacIntyre Snr., at the A.G.M. was to get approval for an increase in subscriptions. After a lengthy discussion the increases were agreed at £6 to £9 for locals and £4 to £5 for visiting gents and £2 to £3 for ladies. His next major duty was much more pleasant as he accepted the new Kildalton Cross from Mrs. Paterson.

By the end of the year the Mackie Quaich had been replaced by White Horse Distillers Ltd. The connection with P.J. Mackie's company had been maintained (see Chapter 9) although the trophy had been renamed as the White Horse Trophy.

The final hurdle of replacing the Foreland Trophy took a little longer to clear. There was no further progress in 1971 when the Hon. Secretary, Ralph Middleton, resigned to move to a new post in Montrose. In appreciation of his 12 years in this position he was presented with a clock. However, the following year his successor, R. Grant, reported that, very appropriately, the new Foreland Trophy had been donated by Tim Morrison, a grandson of the original donor, Wm. Walker. As a sequel to this the club gained an extra trophy when John Callow gifted the Kildalton Plate.

The mystery of what happened to the trophies remains. It would be sacrilege if the silver ones had been melted down although the general consensus was that they were too hot to handle and were hidden or lost in the peat bogs. Some credence was given to this opinion in August 1982 when a shooting party out on the moors found the badly damaged Marshall Trophy. The police were out again combing the area with metal detectors but without success.

A further series of niggling problems beset the Club in the early 1970s. It was proving difficult to get a long term commitment to the post of Hon. Secretary. When J. McGregor was elected at the A.G.M. in 1975 he was the fourth Secretary since 1971. These were troubled times financially as some £1800 was spent on fencing, new mower, tractor and new clubhouse. A further £200 was needed for road repairs for which the local authority refused a grant but instead gave £500 towards the clubhouse. The ladies also offered to help financially but in spite of these factors an overdraft situation arose which resulted in subscription increases for the 1976 season, to £12 for local and £7.50 for visiting males, and £4 for ladies and juniors. A new category for pensioners appeared at £5. It was a long drawn out A.G.M. in 1975 as Mr. McGregor had to cope with proposals and counter proposals on the rules for balls hitting the fences round the greens. His report concluded that 'so far as can be determined the present local rule remains in force. The Secretary apologises if the foregoing appears confused but so was he!'

The Morrison Era

The connection between Islay golf and the whisky industry which was present in the early years through John Ramsay and P.J. Mackie had been re-established in 1970 when Messrs. Lang and Gray bought the hotel and golf course from Bert Marshall. The long established family business of Lang Brothers were wine merchants. When they became part of the Robertson and Baxter Group in 1965 the third generation of the family was still in the company. In 1976 they also bought Glengoyne Distillery. When it was decided to sell the hotel, course and farm it was not unexpected that another family from the whisky industry with a long association with the Islay G.C. should become the new owners in 1976.

The new owner was S.P. Morrison, whisky brokers, blenders and distillers. The founder, Stanley P. Morrison was a scratch golfer for 30 years playing at various times out of Prestwick, Turnberry and Glasgow Golf Clubs. Business took him to Islay in the 1920s and 30s when he was a regular member of Islay G.C. He competed in the Western Isles Open in 1935 and was twice runner up in the Kildalton Cross.

The company was formed as whisky brokers in 1951 by Stanley in partnership with accountant, James Howat, who was also a golfer. They soon expanded into blending before taking a major step forward into distilling in 1963 with the purchase of Bowmore Distillery. It was an intuitive impulsive decision sparked off by a chance remark overheard by Stanley about the impending sale of the distillery to a Spanish Company the following day. By the evening a deal was finalised with a relieved seller who hadn't been too happy to see ownership go overseas. Next morning he phoned his young accountant on holiday on Islay to suggest he should come back quickly as they had just bought a 184 year old distillery.

It was a bold move well timed at the start of the 60s boom years for the whisky industry. Glengarioch Distillery was also bought in 1970 but unfortunately Stanley P. Morrison died the following year. His sons, Tim and Brian, along with James Howat, continued his policy of expansion. Auchentoshan Distillery was purchased in 1984 with the result that by 1986, the company was the highest exporter of bulk malt whisky in Scotland. Diversification into golf came in 1976 with the purchase of the Machrie Hotel, golf course and farm by Machrie Developments Ltd., a subsidiary of Stanley P. Morrison.

The Club's problems disappeared in June 1976 when a meeting was held with the new owners represented by S.W.(Tim) Morrison, A.F. Ross and the hotel manager Rod Walker. Terms were quickly agreed and put to the members by the Captain, J. Callow, at the A.G M. on 2nd August. It was a momentous day for the Islay Golf Club with 59 members present, almost double that for the previous year. The terms were generous. The Club were to be relieved of all responsibility for maintaining the course and all debts including the £600 overdraft would be paid by Machrie Developments Ltd. In return the Club would hand over all mowers, tractors, and fencing, in fact everything except the clubhouse which would stay in their possession. The motion for acceptance was proposed by Lachie

Mackinnon, seconded by W. Soutter and passed unanimously. Opinions were expressed that the local Committee had taken the best possible action on the take over of the course and R. Gibb stated that Tim Morrison was doing his best both for Islay Golf Club and the course. In reply, Tim stated that there would always be liaison with the Club.

Normal business continued as the financial year end was changed to 30th June, a membership fee of the Golf Club was agreed at £1, and D. Stone was elected Hon. Treasurer on the retiral of D. Keith. Rod Walker and Tim Morrison were elected to Committee. With a single stroke the Club's financial problems had been resolved, the work load on the administrators had been considerably reduced and, perhaps the biggest bonus of all, the farm livestock were to be sold. No more fencing round greens, no torn trousers, no need to shoo cows off the line of the shot to the green, and no need for local rules for balls landing in the cow patches.

One problem remained concerning the final payment for the builder work for the new clubhouse started in 1973. After a long drawn out saga the Club's final increased offer of £448 in settlement was accepted in 1978. By this time, Tim Morrison had detailed his plans for the upgrading of the course. Perimeter fencing had been completed, turf specialists had been consulted and a 5 year programme begun for improvement of greens and fairways. Major course alterations were also planned resulting from the decision that the Kintra tenancy would not be renewed. Regrettably it meant the end of Mount Zion, the most famous feature of the links, a hole which the great Harry Vardon feared and respected enough to describe it as the most difficult hole in the world he had ever seen.

Machrie Developments Ltd. planned to spend some £30,000 on the golf course so it was inevitable that some of this would be reflected in the subscriptions. Their first proposals for a 66 per cent increase were not favourably received. The Committee suggested reduced subscriptions of £20 and £12.50 for local gents and ladies respectively which were agreed but there were no reductions for mainland members at £15 and £10. These subscriptions were payable to Machrie Developements Ltd., but the agreed entrance fee of £15 (payable by mainland members only) accrued to the Golf Club.

As the Morrison era dawned with the start of the course improvements, work also began on the refurbishment of the Machrie Hotel. At the same time the Islay Golf Club also entered into a new era.

Wielding a New Broom

In these times of change the Golf Club were not slow to react when, in September 1977, the Captain, John Mason, suggested that the Islay Golf Club needed a proper Constitution since there was none in existence. Douglas Calder, with help from Tim Morrison, was given the task and the final version was approved at the 1978 A.G.M.

On the playing side a trophy was purchased for an annual inter-club match with Lochgilphead G.C. The first match was played at Machrie. Another match was planned at Lochgilphead for the next year but the Committee on reflection cancelled it as they thought it would be difficult to muster sufficient members because of the England v Scotland football match the previous day!

The year of 1977 also saw the introduction of golf weeks when two were held with the professional David Huish in attendance. They were repeated the following year by Machrie Developments with Bill Lockie and Bill Murray giving the lessons. The event proved very popular and remained a fixture for several years.

Other changes were made which saw the introduction of a £1 entry fee for the Kildalton Cross with qualifying for same to be over 36 holes. The Club were pleased also to support by letter the application by Machrie Hotel for an all day licence. The Captain had experienced a busy year, summarised by his successor, John Morrison, at the A.G.M.:

> 'He was greatly indebted to John Mason who had wielded a new broom with astounding efficiency and had left the affairs of the club in first class order.'

The Ladies

The ladies were encouraged to participate more when the Eliot and May Soutter Trophy was presented by the Soutter family in 1965 for a mixed foursomes competition to mark 50 years of family connection with the Islay G.C. The ladies were certainly more involved in the Club now than ever before but as yet there had been no moves to form an official Ladies' Section.

During the early 1970s the Ladies' Section belatedly began to be recognised as fully fledged Associates of the Islay Golf Club. It was suggested in the Minutes of June 1973 that they should 'as a Club apply to join the L.G.U.' The subject was due for discussion at the next A.G.M. but wasn't mentioned in the Minutes. However, their presence and valuable contribution to the club was recognised the following year when it was suggested associateship could only come via an A.G.M. Once again the question wasn't raised and they deservedly slipped into being an unofficial accredited Ladies' Section. The ambitious ladies wanted something the men didn't have namely, practice nets. Captain Bill Sime approved because they had done so much work for the club but he couldn't get the members to agree. They considered there was plenty of room on the course to practise!

To help communications, the ladies were offered a 'spokesman' at the next meeting but only after the official business. When the ladies offered £200 towards the cost of the new clubhouse they soon got their practice mat and net and the ladies' tees were completed. As their membership increased they were being repeatedly praised for their fund-raising efforts. In 1976, the retiring Captain, J. Callow, thanked the ladies 'for creating a new and exciting interest in the Club'. The new owners, Machrie Developments Ltd., were keen to encourage more involvement of the ladies. The hotel manager, Rod Walker, proposed that there should be one lady on Committee but it was overwhelmingly defeated. The new Captain, John Mason, clarified the position at the A.G.M.: 'Ladies are not eligible for Committee by dint of being Associate members only.' However, that wasn't the end of the matter. The full Ladies' Committee were invited to be present at the end of a normal Committee meeting at which Mrs. Earl, their Vice-President, increased their offer to £300 towards the new clubhouse. It was gratefully received. The outcome of this meeting was the promise that a Liaison Committee would be set up to help keep them in the picture and to allow them to air their views.

When the new Club Constitution was approved in August 1978, the Ladies' Section was finally officially brought into the fold. The first Liaison Committee met in February 1979 when the ladies were represented by Mrs. Donalda McFarlane, Lady President, Mrs. Sheena MacMillan, Hon. Secretary and Mrs. Susie Currie. It had taken a long time to get to this stage. Since then the Ladies' Section has continued to flourish although latterly with fewer regular local ladies participating throughout the year.

Course Improvements

Machrie Developments Ltd. commissioned Souter of Stirling (Sports Turf) Ltd. to carry out the reconstruction work on the course to the general design of Donald Steel of the golf course architects, Cotton, Pennink, Lawrie & Partners Ltd. The construction work was controlled by agronomist, John Souter, who was also responsible for the specification and supervision of a five year programme of annual treatment to improve the course and eliminate all weeds from green, tees and fairways. He was impressed by his first sight of the Machrie Links noting that, 'contrary to what one would expect, the potential of the area as a test of golf and as a Greenkeepers' paradise is most exciting'. In particular, he was delighted to find throughout the course the presence of the highly desirable indigenous grass varieties of bent fescue. His initial report stated that, because of the prolonged lack of cultural attention, 'the green areas contain a wide range of weeds; yarrow, daisy, buttercup, poverty shown by moss, dog lichen(peltiga canina) and field woodrush'. Surface/root thatch was also a problem as was the run down state of the Club's machinery.

The new course layout incorporated new holes 10, 11 and 12 at Glenegedale which replaced those lost at Kintra. The 12th hole, 'New Mount Zion' is a fine par 3 but without the severe intimidation factor of its historic namesake. Alterations were also made to holes 13 and 14 and these 5 new holes were brought into play, without ceremony, in July 1979. The improvements impressed Roddie Mackenzie, who wrote from Edinburgh that:

> 'I have never seen the whole course in such good condition. The greens in particular are excellent and free from blemish. There was not one rabbit to be seen.

He gave credit for the improvement to Duncan MacCalman who had returned the previous year to be head greenkeeper after the resignation of D. McNeill. John Souter specified Duncan's workload for the 1979-80 winter to include widening fairways at 11, 13 and 14, manicuring the dog legs at 13 and 14, building new tees at 3 and 8 and re-siting of the 2nd green.

The Score in the Eighties

The pre-Centenary period was one of continued improvements in the quality of the course, upward spiralling subscriptions, the upmarket trend of the 19th hole and another change of landlord. On the down side there was the loss of several long-standing supporters of the Golf Club.

The issue of raised subscriptions also reared its head again. The subscription notice issued by Machrie in March 1980 showed a 20 per cent rise all round, attributed to the rampant inflation of that time. The agreed rates were, local gents £30, ladies £20 with £24 and £18 respectively for mainland members. In the accompanying newsletter, Tim Morrison indicated that the course reconstruction work was now complete except for raising the 2nd fairway to minimise flooding and the re-positioning of the 18th green. He also paid tribute to Duncan MacCalman who was due to retire at the end of the month, aged 72:

> 'Finally and most importantly, I would like to extend my sincere thanks to Duncan MacCalman who has done wonders on the course since he rejoined us. I greatly appreciate his help and the untiring long hours he put into Machrie.'

His replacement was one of the new school of technically qualified young greenkeepers, Jim Paton, from Helensburgh Golf Club, who was a graduate from Auchencruive in Horticulture and Agronomy. However, Duncan's boundless energy was being missed and within a year Paton asked John Souter to re-employ him part-time as 'he was too experienced an asset to lose'.

Initially the new owners concentrated their efforts on upgrading the run down Machrie Hotel. By the time the work on the course was complete, the hotel was completely refurbished with en-suite facilities in many bedrooms, a new Byre Restaurant and a golfers' bar. In addition 15 self-catering cottages were built to meet a growing demand for less expensive family accommodation. The quality and variety of the cuisine also improved considerably so that all aspects of the complex were on a much higher level than before.

Some of the Islay G.C. members felt that they were paying for the course reconstruction by another £5 subscription increase in March 1981. They were soon silenced when Machrie Developments Ltd. pointed out they were getting better value for money than ever before as subscription income only met one quarter of the running costs of the course. 1981 also saw the departure of Rod Walker who was replaced by Mr. and Mrs. Ted Hiram from the Bridgend Hotel, Islay.

With all work completed on the course and in the hotel, Tim Morrison embarked on an extensive marketing campaign reminiscent of the early years of the Club. The late Pat Ward Thomas, a prominent golf writer was considered by many to be the natural successor to the great Bernard Darwin who in his later years regretted his failure to visit Islay. Pat did not make the same mistake and recorded his findings in an article published in *Country Life*, entitled 'Finding Enchantment on Islay'. He wrote:

'Wherever the game be played the golfer has a sense of freedom from the tribulations and ugliness of the everyday world. Rarely have I been aware of this as at Machrie ...Now cattle and sheep no longer share the Links with the golfers, who face what can be a pleasure for the humble and at the same time a rare challenge for the best if the wind be firm.'

The publicity campaign continued as Donald Steel, who was also golf correspondent of *The Sunday Telegraph,* had at least two articles published. 'Machrie's Many Splendours' appeared in a new book, *The Golf Course Guide to the British Isles.* Like all writers before him he was impressed by the remoteness of the course with its natural links setting and commented on the new holes:

'Some of the eccentricities that grew up before there was much in the way of machinery or golf course architects have been reduced; gone are one or two, though not all, of the blind shots into crater greens - a type of hole not so favourably looked upon as it once was: and in their place have arisen a new 2nd, 10th, 11th, 12th 13th and 14th that offer in distillers' language, a smoother blend.'

He could also have quoted a Bowmore Whisky advert from the 1890s, 'Flaghinn agus Soir Bhuanaqhadl', which in Islay Gaelic means 'Full and excellent quality'.

In his second article, 'A Question of Design' which appeared in the October 1981 issue of *Greenkeeper*, he complimented Tim Morrison for his decision to eliminate Mount Zion and gave himself a pat on the back: 'the redesign combines the best of both ancient and modern worlds', a sentiment with which most golfers would agree. The redesign produced finally a measured length of 6226 yards and a S.S.S. of 69. An application to the S.G.U. for an extra one for difficulty was approved in 1982. The ladies circuit now had proper tees throughout and was measured at 5210 yards.

By 1982, gents and ladies subscriptions had taken another substantial jump up the inflation ladder to £48.30 and £35.65 respectively with mainland members at £40.25 and £35.20 respectively all inclusive of 15 per cent V.A.T. and the club subscription of £1.

The arrival of Machrie Developments and Tim Morrison in particular heralded a new interest in the encouragement of junior golfers from the local schools. Juniors under 16 were allowed free golf, no entrance fee and membership of the golf club for £1. The company also gave a junior trophy for competition during Cross week. Boy caddies were also given a good deal when fees were fixed at £1.50 per round and £3 per day. In 1982, a Junior coaching scheme was started with regular competitions. A very generous offer by Tim saw the boy and girl winners taken for a two day trip to the Open whenever it was held in Scotland. Only two girls entered the competition in 1982 so both were invited to enjoy a visit to Troon including accommodation and flight by courtesy of Loganair, 'Scotland's Airline' which brings us to its managing director, Scott Grier.

He was Captain of the Club and in his retiring speech in August 1982 he was pleased to report that the three Mackinnon brothers, Alex, Dugie and Lachie were all back together competing in the Kildalton Cross. Sadly, he also reported the death of past captain, Malcolm McNeill, who had 'amongst his many attributes unfailingly enlivened Annual General Meetings over a period of some 25 years'. The new Captain, Jim MacFarlane, commented favourably on the state of the course: 'there had been a transformation of the golf course. Gone were the days when cattle roamed freely and many a fine shot firmly embedded in a Hovis Brown.'

Early in 1983 the Committee were concerned that the high subscriptions would be a deterrent to members who only came over at Cross week. The ladies also were afraid that the success of their new active Ladies' Section could be in danger. Before their fears could be settled it was announced that the hotel and course had been leased out to Murdo MacPherson, former manager of the Aviemore Centre. A colossal sum had been spent by Machrie Developments on the Hotel and course which considerably enhanced the fine reputation of the Machrie, but possibly there had been insufficient time to see it developed to its full potential.

When Murdo took over in March, subscriptions for the year ahead still had to be negotiated. He responded to the fears of the Committee by agreeing to keep the subscriptions unchanged, except for the local ladies who 'mirabile dictu' got a £4.35 reduction. The Club Constitution was then changed to allow those paying green fees for one or two weeks to join the Club.

John Souter completed his advisory contract but having joined the Golf Club, he was still around and generously gave donations of £15 and £50 for the benefit of the juniors. Another result of his presence was the formation of the 'Machrie Misfits', a group of golfers who paid an annual pilgrimage to Islay for a long weekend of golf, more golf and maybe a drink or two. Members included Tim Morrison, John Edgar and Alastair Connell, course manager of Cawder G.C.

With Murdo MacPherson now on the Committee, Tim Morrison resigned. His letter to Hon. Secretary, Douglas Stone concluded thus:

'I would also like to say that I thoroughly enjoyed the meetings although the mornings after were sometimes fraught with a haziness which made total recall of the previous evening's business merely an imagination until the Secretary's notes were relayed later!'

Iain Middleton would have no bother remembering his score on 30th July 1983 in the Club Championship when he established a new course record of 66 as follows:-

$$4\ 4\ 4, 4\ 3\ 4, 3\ 4\ 4 = 34 \quad \text{and} \quad 2\ 3\ 3, 5\ 3\ 4, 4\ 3\ 5 = 32$$

His only deviation over par came at the last but 6 birdies ensured a record which should stand for many years to come.

According to George Orwell writing in earlier years from the seclusion of the Isle of Jura the record would only stand for one year as he forecast that 1984 would see the end of the world. His thoughts on golf weren't quite accurate either. He disapproved of the tendency for golf and lawn tennis to take precedence over cricket and wrote:

'There can be no doubt that this is a disaster for these games are not only inferior aesthetically to cricket but they do not have the socially binding quality that cricket at any rate used to have.....the inherently Scottish game is golf which causes whole stretches of countryside to be turned into carefully guarded class preserves.'

It was certainly no doom and gloom year for the Golf Club as agreement was reached with Murdo for a modest 10 per cent increase in all subscriptions. The highlight of the year came with the news that triple Open Champion, Henry Cotton, had been persuaded to visit Islay after the Open at St Andrews. Henry's godson, Tim Morrison, had been trying for years to get him to play at Machrie so it was quite a scoop. It had been 83 years since the previous triple Open Champions Vardon and Taylor stepped on to the Machrie turf. Cotton won his Opens in 1934, 1937 and 1948 and undoubtedly would have won more but for the Second World War. Now 72 years old he played round Machrie riding on an electric buggy and held some teaching clinics. The sale of old rubber car tyres would have increased on Islay as he expounded his pet theory for strengthening the wrists - strike the tyre repeatedly with the club head, keeping the wrists firm.

Sadly, 1984 also saw the sudden death of Duncan MacCalman while still employed as part-time assistant greenkeeper, aged 76. Two years later, Douglas Stone resigned after 10 years as Hon. Secretary/Treasurer to be followed by the news that Murdo MacPherson now owned the hotel and golf course. The effect on the Golf Club of the change was significant. A sympathetic landlord with readily available back-up from the parent company had been replaced by an individual owner whose first priority had to be to keep his bankers happy. Murdo had purchased a fine historic course in top condition after an unprecedented eight years of modern greenkeeping treatment. This condition was maintained and arguably improved under the care of Murdo and his head greenkeeper D. Woodburn. This factor without doubt helped to ease the pain of the annual subscription increases. The annual negotiations gradually became more difficult and protracted as the two factions tried to balance the need to show a profit on one side with the possibility of losing both local and mainland members if the subscriptions were too high.

In 1988 one-day 'High Flying Golfing Trips to Islay' were introduced by Murdo and Loganair. They were priced very economically and proved very popular with golf parties. However they weren't too popular with the local inhabitants as on occasions there were so many golfers and their baggage that there was no room for the daily newspapers which were relegated to a later arrival by ferry or the next plane. Golf parties were limited eventually to 12.

As the 1988 golf season drew to a close there was sad news for the Islay Golf Club. First came the death of Lachie Mackinnon, a real character of the club, former Committee member and a first class golfer. As the representative of the Mid-Argyll Tourist Board he helped to set up the first golf week at Machrie with professionals in attendance. In his memory the family presented the Mackinnon Memorial Trophy which is a handicap prize on Club Championship day. A second loss came with the death of Mrs. M.S. Paterson, the generous donor of the replacement Kildalton Cross.

Loganair "High Flying Golfing Trip"

The "Cross" winner in 1990, John F. Mason, rt., with his father John A., also a "Cross" winner and his grandfather.

A link with the original Kildalton Cross came in 1989 when the family of the late S.W. Thompson presented to the Club the replica Cross which he won in 1926. It has been suggested that he was possibly the first Englishman to win the Kildalton Cross. The replica is now the target of the over-50s on club championship days.

The Junior Golf Section was thriving with great encouragement from the Golf Club and Murdo. Still enjoying free golf in the 1988/89 season, they played 12 monthly medals and competed for 6 trophies. D. Turner came out on top in the medals with 7 wins to 3 for S Crawford but the roles were reversed in the trophy competitions. The latter won Ernie's Challenge, the Junior Club Championship and the Loganair Trophy compared with Turner winning the Royal Bank of Scotland Trophy and the Laphroaig Trophy. The Morrison Shield was won by C. Holyoake. The juniors weren't forgotten about in Cross week either as they had their own Junior Cross competitions, both scratch and handicap, for visitors and locals. In an article in the *Ileach,* the Junior Section Secretary, Dianne Brown, thanked all the contributors, Tim Morrison and Scott Grier for the trip to the Open, Mr. and Mrs. MacPherson for all they had done for the junior golfers and the greenkeeper, David Woodburn, who has been marvellous in keeping the course in tip-top condition.

February 1990 saw the first meeting of the Centenary Committee at which Murdo announced that he was arranging an author and printer for a Centenary publication. A month later Tom Dunn took over as interim Secretary/ Treasurer after the resignation of Drew Hyslop. By the autumn the Club decided to purchase a special Centenary cabinet to house the club trophies. The order was placed with D. Renshaw, a local cabinet maker with a very high reputation for quality workmanship. The funding came from an anonymous donation. The plans of the Islay Golf Club were unfolding for the Centenary celebrations which are worthy of a separate chapter.

The run up to the Centenary produced some major changes, not the least being the loss by the Golf Club, of responsibility for course upkeep. With hindsight it proved a good move as finance became available, where none had been before, to upgrade the course and maintain it to a high standard unknown in earlier years. It did not come cheaply as subscriptions raced upwards after each annual lengthy negotiations on the annual fee. Common sense and compromise generally prevailed but not without some loss of faith and confidence on both sides. However, golf prevailed as the wheels were set in motion for the Centenary celebrations to which both parties were fully committed.

Club Trophies.

CHAPTER EIGHT

THE KILDALTON CHALLENGE CROSS

Early Cross Days

A new challenge trophy for the Islay golfers was an ideal way to celebrate the start of the twentieth century. It was also another factor in the ongoing publicity campaign to encourage more and more visitors from afar to help achieve success for both the Golf Club and the hotel. When the Ramsay family presented the Kildalton Challenge Cross to the Golf Club neither they nor the Club officials could have realised that they had just created the lifeline on which the future of the Islay Golf Club would depend.

The first competition for the prestigious silver Kildalton Challenge Cross was fixed for 8th August 1900. It was advertised three times in each of *The Glasgow Herald* and *The Scotsman* newspapers and twice in Golf.

Four days before the Cross, Miss Ramsay presented a silver match box for competition. The Rev. James E. Pease gave notice of his golfing skills by winning it with a score of 85+1 = 86. His good form continued into the Cross and it was most appropriate that the Reverend became the first winner. He didn't defend his title the following year, possibly because of a late decision by the Committee on 10th July to advertise that the competition would now be held in the third week of August. There were 29 competitors including 4 from the Evans family. It was a successful week for E.D. Evans (scratch) who beat J. Buchanan by 1 hole in the 36 hole final. Local members were in the minority, there being only six of them in the first draw. Peter Reid (9) was the local back marker out of the 20 locals who had handicaps.

The Rev. J.E. Pease was back again in 1902, now with a +2 handicap and won the 30th July Medal with a gross score of 79, six below the scratch score of 85. He didn't enter for the Cross. However, another prominent golfing family appeared,

The original Kildalton Challenge Cross.

the Lambies, who had 3 players of handicaps scratch to 4. W.A. Lambie (scratch) was the winner in the final against J.B. Fishwick.

By the following year, the tradition of making Cross week a family golfing holiday could be said to have been established. The three Lambies were again present, joined by three from the Mackay clan. The scratch men prevailed as three of them reached the penultimate stage. The custom of the times was to allow both players in a tied match to go into the draw for the next round. As a result three names went into the hat for the last draw. They were A.M. McAdam, R.G. Mackay and L. Mackay. The latter got a bye into the final and went on to victory although it is not clear who his opponent was.

After another scratch man, A. McVean was successful in 1904 by defeating A.M. Lambie (4) by 2 and 1, it was the turn of the handicap golfer in 1905 to change the pattern. The total entry had risen to 48 including 3 scratch and 3 plus handicaps. Ron McArthur and Peter Reid survived to the 3rd round where Reid lost to J.E. Murray (18), the eventual winner. Murray was fortunate to get a bye into the semi-final but never went beyond the 15th green in any match. He didn't re-appear in the following years to find out how much his handicap had been slashed!

The year 1906 saw the first Islay winner Percy Bolland (8) beating A.S. Wedderburn by 5 and 4 in the final. Prior to the final, the shock of the week was the defeat of a previous winner, A. McVean (+1), in the third round by the Club Treasurer, J. Bolland (15). 'I don't believe it' would have been the loser's comments as he mused on his 10 and 8 defeat. This year also saw for the first time the introduction of a 'hole by hole' competition for losers in the early rounds of the Cross. The winner of the special prize presented by Miss Ramsay was F. W. Kennedy, the back marker at +2, who had been eliminated from the Cross by Percy Bolland.

F.W. Kennedy from Glasgow was back again the following year along with J. S. Kennedy (scratch). By a strange coincidence they both met in the third round, the result being a halved match. Fate brought them together again in the final which was won by J. S. Kennedy.

A new Islay star had arrived on the course at this time, Malcolm MacIntyre. He was given his first handicap of 20 which had been cut to 6 a year later as he entered his first ever Cross in 1908. It had now been moved to the first week in August when there were 9 scratch golfers in a field of 44. MacIntyre disposed of one of them in the 4th draw before he met another in the final, A.C. Hamilton from Maidenhead. They finished all square over 36 holes before the experienced Hamilton won the replay by 2 and 1.

Two members of the Albany Club in Edinburgh who were probably related reached the final in 1909 when C.A. Macpherson (scratch) triumphed by 2 and 1 over Dr. L. Macpherson (+1).

A rare feat was achieved the following year when the current Captain of the Islay Golf Club, P.D. Hendry (8), won the Cross beating Dr. McLarty (7) by 3 and 2. The honours went north in 1911 when the winner was A.W. Mitchell from Royal Aberdeen G.C.

However, the standard of Islay golf was improving as its star local member Malcolm MacIntyre, now up to 2 from scratch the previous year, gave the club its second victory in 1912. The third came the following year when S. Percy Bolland won again. The fame of the Machrie had certainly spread as his opponent was A. Clarke (scratch) from Ceylon. Islay golfers had certainly come to the fore, a fact which was reinforced the following year when the back marker was McIntyre at +2. It wasn't too great a burden for him as he again reached the final before losing by 3 and 2 to J.S. Graham (scratch) from Edinburgh. This was the last Cross to be played until after the war.

The Cross, Post-War

The stars of the 1920 Cross competition included P. E. Soutter and H. G. Isitt both scratch, John McBean(+1) and J. Stanley Graham (+2). Graham, the 1914 winner, would have been the favourite. However, he met his match when P.E.Soutter (P.E.S.) beat him by 7 and 6 for his first win. This earned 'P.E.S.' the statutory 2 shot reduction in handicap. It didn't stop his successes in the following week when he was runner up to L. R. Hamilton in the Machrie Quaich. The competition for the Cross increased the following year with the appearance of another 3 scratch players, J. L. Wilson, H.G. Hendry and the 1908 winner, A. C. Hamilton. A repeat Graham v Soutter final was expected but Hendry had other ideas as he beat 'P.E.S.' by 3 and 2 to join Graham in the final. A similar score gave Graham his second Cross victory.

In the midst of protracted negotiations for a new lease with the new proprietor, Mr. Hindle, it was decided to celebrate the 25th anniversary of the start of the Cross tournament by holding special competitions during the week following the 1924 event. For the first time, the increasing popularity forced the introduction of an 18 hole qualifying round with 32 qualifiers. The Captain, P.E. Soutter, proposed that on this occasion the club should entertain the members and friends to tea. Up until 1921, the results of all matches in the Cross were meticulously recorded in the Minute book. After Mr. Etoe became Hon. Secretary and Treasurer in 1922, only the results of the final were noted in the Minutes but excluding the 1924 result. However, an intensive seach by the author produed the result. J.S.

Graham (Bruntsfield) beat C.J. Morris (Nottingham City) to become the first triple winner of the Kildalton Cross.

A newspaper cutting which survived in the Minute book gives full details of the 'Islay Golfing Week' from Monday 3rd August to Saturday 8th August 1925. Bogey competitions were held on the first two days followed by the Cross qualifying on the Wednesday, now over 36 holes. P.E. Soutter gave the prize for the leading qualifier who was A. White. A large crowd watched the final when M.R. Armstrong (Erskine) beat R.M. Struthers (Pollock),'after a stubborn fight'. The consolation handicap competition for those knocked out was won by A.W. Pollock with Mr.Etoe equal third. It was a successful week for Mr. Etoe as he won the Captain's prize and then the mixed foursomes with Dr. Isa Robertson. After the prize-giving, Mr. H. Bisset, who was leaving the island after many years on Committee, was presented with a handsome clock.

Rule Changes and Cross Domination

The 1925 report stated that many games went beyond the 20th hole indicating a change from the original rule which allowed ties to proceed to the next draw. Further changes came in February 1930 when the Committee decided that in the event of a tie in the Cross, 3 extra holes should be played, 'with stroke handicap', and if still undecided another three holes and so on until the tie was won. The prime mover in all matters of administration, playing conditions and rule changes for many years was P.E. Soutter. At the 1930 A.G.M. he successfully proposed that the Cross qualifying be reduced back to 18 holes and that the maximum handicap be 12. However, the tinkering with the Cross rules was not over. In 1932 the rules for ties were again changed to 6 extra holes instead of 3, then another 3 and if still all square, 'thereafter one hole to decide the match'. The following year the date was changed to coincide with the Glasgow Fair holiday in July. This wasn't a success so it reverted to its traditional early August date the following year.

The remarkable feature of the Kildalton Cross competition during the 1930s decade was its domination by the names Soutter and MacGregor. P.E. Soutter gained his second victory in 1932 a feat which was equalled by his son P.E. Soutter Jnr. with wins in 1937 and 1939. J.B. Soutter also won in 1936 but they had to give way to their rivals when Roy C. MacGregor was successful in 1933 and 1935 and his brother Jimmy won in 1934. After the war the domination continued as before when J.B. Soutter won the first post-war event to be followed by P.E. Soutter Jnr. in 1949. This was a remarkable achievement for P.E. Soutter Jnr. as it meant he was the second person to win the Cross three times. Roy C. MacGregor now a Scottish Internationalist then took over, winning in 1950 and 1951, to become

"Cross" Presentation in 1920's. Dr. Chadborn (Captain 1929-30) in centre of table then, seated, Captain Iain Ramsay, P. E. Soutter Snr., and Col. M. MacTaggart, D. C. McIntyre stg. to rt.

"Cross" Presentation, 1928. At table l to rt., winner R. M. Struthers, John McBean (Captain 1928-29) and Mr. Etoe. D. C. McIntyre, cr. standing and John McMillan head greenkeeper at doorway. Donald McLachlan ex headmaster of Port Ellen school on extreme right.

"Cross" Presentation, 1929/30. At table l to rt., winner R. M. Munro, Dr. Chadborn, P. E. Soutter Snr., Mr. Etoe.

The "Cross" final, 1935.

only the second person to successfully defend the Cross and the only person ever to achieve four victories. The latter year was unique for two reasons. An entry fee of 2/6d was introduced for the first time to help meet the cost of the replicas given to each winner and ladies became eligible to play in the Cross provided they had an L.G.U. handicap with a maximum of 12.

Not to be outdone, the Secretary, Alec Mackinnon, followed suit with wins in 1952 and 1953. An unprecedented third successive win was a possibility the next year but Alec lost in the final to D. McDougall by one hole. The story of his battle in the final of 1953 against E. Watt is told in a poem written by Alistair Balfour Sinclair, a mainland member. The copy came from Alec.

The Battle of Kildalton Cross

They met upon the Machrie course
Amongst the heather and the gorse
The proud Mackinnon and valiant Watt
Fierce Highlandman and Lowland Scot
No broadswords here, or targets bright,
Nor Fiery Cross by dead of night.
No pibroch sounding in the glen,
To stir the blood of Highlandmen.

For many a year, the Islay mists,
Have welcomed all the lists,
And there upon the heather and the moss,
The prize, the famed Kildalton Cross.
To bravely strive with might and main,
This precious relic to attain,
And by the wayside lie the dead,
Who found Machrie no rosy bed.

So girt for battle, they strode forth,
The Lowland South and Highland North,
And all the ghosts of longtime past,
Lined the holes from first to last,
On Laggan Bay, the waves stood still,
Enraptured by pure golfing skill,
And Eagles in their awesome flight,
Swooped down to watch the doughty fight.
With lunge and parry, club and ball,
Naught could shake the Highland wall.

The long day through, they fought apace,
With all the courage of their race,
And Angels from the Heaven's above,
Came riding down on backs of dove.
They spoke in Gaelic, not strange to tell,
No other tongue would suit as well.
With walkie talkies in their hands,
They swooped about in roving bands.
Relayed the news to their dear Lord,
Of how it stood on Machrie sward.

> And up in Heaven, the dear Lord said,
> At last the long day drew its blinds,
> The Lowland Scot was far behind,
> A gallant fighter brave and true,
> As good as any Machrie knew.
> Thank God for Alec, I'm off to bed.

The 1958 final between John MacIntyre Snr. and Jimmy McGregor caused quite a few headaches for the Committee when the match finished all square after 36 holes. John, several holes up with 9 to play had his confidence shattered as his opponent suddenly in desperation couldn't do anything wrong and squared the game at the last. Nobody was sure what came next. Sudden death or another 18 holes or even 36? Secretary, Ralph Middleton, had a quick Committee meeting - no decision. They telephoned former Secretary, Mr. Etoe - still no decision. It was then left to the players to decide. Jimmy opted for 36 holes to which John, still suffering from the birdie and par onslaught, was relieved to agree. After a few drams and a good nights sleep John was ready for the fray and won 11 and 9.

The Ladies and the Cross

The ladies had been allowed to play in the Cross since 1951. In order to encourage their participation in the 'Cross', Mr. Lang reminded the members at the A.G.M. in 1962 that they were still eligible to play. The newly appointed Captain, Mr. A. McNeil, immediately proposed that this rule be eliminated. The motion was passed but he then had to face a motion of no confidence in the Captain which was defeated 'amidst much hilarity'.

The Auction and The Cross

The first auction for the names of the Cross qualifiers was proposed by J.B. Soutter at the A.G.M. in 1960. After much discussion with the newly elected Captain, Lachie Mackinnon in the chair, it was approved on condition that 25 per cent of the total auction cash went to the Golf Club and that 'the auction should be run by Hotel members'. The future would prove the importance of the auction in helping to balance the books but not without some serious doubts about its legality in the eyes of the R.& A.

After a long absence from the headlines, the Soutter family returned to the fore with the victory of past Captain Dr.W.P. Soutter in 1962. This meant that each of P.E. Soutter Snr.'s three sons had won the Cross. The following year the rules for deciding tied matches in the Cross were changed to sudden death but with no handicap allowance. The winner this time was Dugie Mackinnon following in the

The "Cross" final, 1935. The Captain, J. Wilson with finalists and Mr. Etoe.

The "Cross" winner of 1935, Roy C. MacGregor, Mrs. D. C. McIntyre holding replica "Cross"

footsteps of brother Alec. He did not have his troubles to seek when he became Captain in 1968, the year the Kildalton Cross and other trophies were stolen. There was no trophy to present to the 1968 and 1969 winners, G. Stevenson and Lachie Mackinnon respectively. The replacement Kildalton Cross, donated by Mrs. M.S. Paterson, was presented to its first winner A.D. MacKenzie in 1970.

The success of the auction continued to be a great boost to club funds. From a modest start of £15, the auction income had risen to £100 in 1966, helped by a re-allocation of the takings to give the club 50 per cent. A further ten fold increase by the year 1977 saw some doubts being expressed by Past Captain Malcolm McNeill about the large sums of money at stake and the possible infringement of amateur status. The fluctuations in the Cross qualifying rules appeared again in 1977 when 36 hole qualifying was brought back and the entry fee increased to £1. Some doubts about the auction were eased with the introduction of a £15 entry fee to the Golf Club for new members who had to be proposed by at least two persons each with a minimum of 3 years membership. By these means it was hoped to discourage those whose only interests were the rich pickings from the auction.

The dominant feature of the Cross results in the late 1970s and early 1980s was the number of multiple winners. Both D. Gray and J.D. Gordon became triple winners and W.Douglas Calder had his second win of the 70s decade. After retiring as Captain in 1984, Douglas was back in the limelight expressing doubts about the validity of the auction relative to the rules of golf. Enquiries to Prestwick G.C. brought the reply that, as their auction was conducted privately among members only, they were not concerned with the rules imposed by St. Andrews. Douglas withdrew his objections to the auction but inevitably the subject could well be raised again in the future. All conditions were unchanged as arrangements were made throughout the world for a special visit to Islay for the Kildalton Cross week in Centenary year.

Cross Week in Centenary Year

Tom Dunn, the Secretary, set the scene in the 'Islay Links' newsletter:

'From Hong Kong and Australia, from Canada and California, Germany and Ireland and even Port Wemyss and Lagavulin they arrived in their dozens to compete or spectate, to meet old friends or make new ones. The camaraderie was such that there was a danger of forgetting what had brought them together - The Kildalton Cross Week - more significant in this, the Club's Centenary year.'

Mount Zion green, 1950s.

The "Cross" winner of 1967, John MacFarlane.

"Cross" Presentation, 1937. At table, l. to rt., D. C. McIntyre, P. E. Souttar Jnr. the winner, Mrs. A. M. Campbell, Dr. A. M. Campbell (Captain 1936-1937), Wm. Aitken Hon. Secretary & Treasurer (standing), J. Wilson, P. E. Souttar Snr., and runner-up, J. A. Cruikshank.

1955/57 "Cross" winner Ian Henderson with his daughter Margery and caddie Gilbert Stevenson.

First event of the week was the Club Championship held over 36 holes in fine weather on Saturday 3rd. August. Iain Middleton from Aberdeen, winner of the Centenary Trophy became Club Champion with a scratch score of 154. Two other handicap competitions were played on the same day, the Mackinnon Memorial Trophy and the J.W. Thompson Cross(over 50s) which were won respectively by Donald Holyoake (136 net) and Syd Durk (38 net for 10 holes). At the evening A.G.M. John MacIntyre Jnr. was elected Captain and thus matched his father's rare feat of a Cross and Captain double.

Sunday was fun day, the visitors v locals match with a shot gun start as usual coming from Murdo MacPherson. The visitors came out on top by 8 to 5 with one halved match. It was back to serious golf on Monday and Tuesday for the two qualifying rounds for the Cross with 79 players. Scoring in the first round was good as Simon Jones, a new member from Dorset won the Captain's prize with a fine net 65 by virtue of a better inward half than I. Middleton. The Peking Cup was at stake on the Tuesday as well as the 32 qualifying places for the Cross. At the end of another perfect day, the cut for the Cross came at 148 net and the Soutter family came back to the fore as Eliot Soutter won the Peking Cup with again a net 65 and a better inward half than R. Kidd. The next 32 qualifiers were scheduled to play a knock out competition for the Kildalton Plate.

Wednesday night is draw and auction night and the punters were spoiled for choice with many of the 'big guns' in the draw and a good mixture of youth and experience. The Club's coaching policy for juniors was paying off as David Turner and Charles Holyoake, both in their first year as seniors, qualified but unfortunately met in the first round, the former being the winner. A further win saw him face up to another Ileach, David Livingstone, in the quarter finals. Other matches included the former winner of the Western Isles Open at Machrie, Jim Unick v Andrew Soutter, Arthur Holyoake v Norman Macdonald both former Cross winners and Bob Hogben v Tim Morrison. Experience proved invaluable as David Livingstone went through to face Jim Unick in the semi-final and Tim's perseverance saw him also through to face Arthur Holyoake. Sentiment dictated Tim's turn for the Cross was long overdue but it wasn't to be as after a close match Arthur won to face his cousin David in the 36 hole final.

Half the handicap difference meant David started 3 up on the first tee which he had increased to 4 after 18 holes, completed in 2 hours 40 minutes. Still 3 up after 9 in the afternoon he couldn't match the 5 successive pars of his opponent which brought the match level. After an interchange of holes the match was still all square after 36. No problems with the play off rules this time, it was sudden

The "Cross" winner of 1970, Alan MacKenzie.

The "Cross" winner of 1981, John Gordon (l) and Scott Grier (Captain 1981-82).

Guests at Centenary Reception.
l to r: J. Cubbage, J. Calder, W. Smith, A. Smith, A. Sinclair, E. Sinclair, O. Cubbage, Belle Robertson, J. R. Best, B. Best, Mr & Mrs A. MacLachlan.

Lagavulin Quaich. Presentation to Ralph Middleton, Captain of Islay Golf Club, by Michael Nicholson the manager of Lagavulin Distillery, Islay, May 1996.

"Cross" winner of 1968, Gilbert Stevenson with Duncan MacCalman.

The "Cross" winner on Centenary Year, 1991, Arthur Holyoake (l) with John MacIntyre Jnr (Captain 1991-92).

By Frazer McArthur

death. Sudden it was, as David failed to hole a short putt at the 37th. This gave Arthur his second victory in the Cross. In the secondary competition for the Kildalton Plate, David Middleton, from Aberdeen, beat local member Thomas Logan.

A memorable week was concluded with a sumptuous dinner in the Machrie Hotel attended by over 120 members and guests. The oldest person present would undoubtedly have been the late Past Captain, Forrest Anderson, 89 years old. The usual lively Ceilidh thereafter continued into the small hours.

The finale came on Saturday morning as the departing golfers and families headed homewards into the care of Loganair or MacBraynes. After an A.G.M., 2 dinners, one dance, one Ceilidh, many a dram and up to 11 rounds of golf comprising a walk of up to 44 miles there were some weary legs but there were no losers. As the fond farewells were made, the spirit of Cross Week echoed round the airport and pier in the parting cries of young and old:

'Beannachd leibh agus coinnichidh sinn aig an at'
'Good-bye until we meet at the Cross next year'

On the First Tee. Bill Smith and John MacIntyre Jnr, followed by Robin and Jan MacGregor.

The Grand Match, Victors and Vanquished.

CHAPTER NINE

SIR PETER JEFFREY MACKIE AND THE MACKIE QUAICH

When ill health forced Peter Jeffrey Mackie to resign as Captain of the Islay Golf Club in 1896, it signalled the end of 6 years of his active membership. The story of his part in the formation of the Golf Club and of the Lagavulin Quaich has already been told. His name is notably absent from the Minute book for the next 17 years other than to record a gift of £2 to the club.

He first visited Islay in 1878 and learned the art of distilling at Lagavulin Distillery under his uncle, James Logan Mackie, who formed Mackie and Company in 1883. By 1891 when the brand name White Horse was registered, Peter was at the helm and eventually purchased other distilleries namely Hazelburn in Kintyre and Craigellachie and Ballindalloch in the north. His many interests included collecting antiques in silver, china, furniture and paintings, in search of which he travelled extensively. Exploration took his fancy and he funded the Mackie Ethnological Expedition to East Africa in 1919 to study and research the previously unknown primitive 'Bakitari' tribe. Thirty years of his life were spent in politics and he took a great interest in all kinds of sport. He was particularly knowledgeable in country sports and along with others wrote The Keepers Book on this subject which was published in 1904. Cricket and golf were in receipt of his generous patronage. Not surprisingly, he was a busy man throughout his life, which possibly explains why he was no longer in the limelight of Islay golf.

In his obituary in 1924, his large business interests on Islay were quoted as was his concern for 'the welfare of the natives of which was a matter in which he took a close personal interest'. It was probably this interest and the increasing popularity of the Machrie Links which encouraged him to offer the Mackie Quaich to the Islay Golf Club for annual competition.

The Mackie Quaich and the White Horse Trophy

The donor spelt out the competition rules. The inscription was to read, 'Presented by P. Jeffrey Mackie, J.P. F.S.A. to Islay Golf Club for Annual Competition, August 1913'. The Committee approved the donor's conditions which were as follows:

'In handing over the 'Mackie Quaich' to the Islay Golf Club I wish the following conditions to be observed. The Trophy is to be played for annually and the Competition is to be open to all members of the Club and is to take the form of two rounds of medal play under handicap. The maximum handicap is to be restricted to 12 strokes from scratch in each round of 18 holes.

The winner in each yearly competition will receive from me a replica of the 'Mackie Quaich' with his name inscribed thereon. The 'Mackie Quaich' itself will become the property of the member who first registers his third victory in the competition.

Gleneasdell, Whitehouse, Argyllshire. 18th. September 1913.
(sgd) P. Jeffrey Mackie.'

The offer was gratefully accepted and the first competition fixed for July 1914, when Dr. Edgar Reid from Swansea became the first winner with nett scores of 86 and 85 playing off two. A few weeks later, at the A.G.M., the members were told of the inscription on the trophy which read :

'The Mackie Quaich. To the Islay Golf Club for annual competition. Presented in 1914 by Peter Jeffrey Mackie, J.P. F.S.A. Scot. of Lagavulin who founded the club in 1891.'

The members present, all 13 of them, unanimously expressed their disagreement and instructed the Secretary to write to Mr. Mackie, pointing out that the subscription should be altered to read '..one of the founders of the club in 1891'.

The final inscription had obviously been altered by Mr. Mackie without consulting the Committee who considered he was taking full credit to the exclusion of several local members who also contributed greatly to the establishment of the Golf Club. Letters passed to and fro until the end of the year without a solution so it was left until the next A.G.M. when it was decided not to play for it until the matter had been resolved. In fact, the matter was carried forward at the two following A.G.M.s 'due to paucity of members present'.

Competitions were cancelled in any event during the war and the unresolved problem seemed to have been forgotten about until 1919 when things were back to normal. The Mackie Quaich competition was fixed for 3rd September, subject to the approval of Mr. Mackie. The letter must have raised the question of the inscription again but Mr. Mackie had mellowed. He replied, 'I quite agree to any decision the Committee may come to.' This reply was added as an afterthought to the Minutes but there was no record of the decision on the inscription.

The first post-war competition in 1919 for the Mackie Quaich was won by Mr. W. Patrick from Glasgow with scores of 83 and 85 playing off 5. The most disappointed player must have been Geo. A. Cook, winner of the Kildalton Cross 10 days previously playing off 5. He finished second last with a nett score of 205. Obviously he had not recovered from the shock of his handicap reduction to one after his triumph.

Competition was really hot the following year when 7 of the 22 players were scratch or better. P.E.Soutter (Scr) winner of the Cross was promptly cut to +2 but still finished runner up in the Quaich to L.R. Hamilton (+2). He went one better the next year, 1921, to win the Quaich, now playing off +3. Judging by the nett scores above, the top players were finding the Machrie Links were pretty tough when compared with the par and scratch of 73 and 78 respectively as submitted in 1922 to the newly formed S.G.U.

Having been made a baronet in 1920, Sir Peter J. Mackie continued his benevolence towards golf in what was probably his last such act in September 1924. An international two day match was arranged at Gleneagles between Scotland and America represented by George Duncan and Macdonald Smith respectively. Over 36 holes Carnoustie born Smith won by 4 and 3. His score of 7 under fours was quite phenomenal for these hickory shaft days. Mackie generously provided prize-money and a Souvenir Cup which was presented by Mrs. G.O.L. Campbell in the absence of her father, Sir P.J. Mackie. He had been ill for some weeks and died three weeks later at home, Corraith, Symington. Not long after his death the company name was changed to White Horse Distillers Ltd. before being sold to Distillers Co. Ltd. in 1927.

Records of the Quaich winners don't seem to have been kept between 1923 and 1935. The format changed to match play for one year, wasn't successful and went back to stroke play over 18 holes until the second world war broke out. It returned in 1948 and 1949 as a bogey competition, being won in 1949 by Alex Mackinnon, Hon. Secretary and Treasurer. The members couldn't make up their minds about the format as it was changed yet again back to the pre-war 18 holes in 1950. Alex (10) was again to the fore only to be beaten by one stroke by his brother, Dugie (8) with a nett 67.

Willie White got his name on the cup in 1952 with a nett 68 before three prominent Islay golfers took command of the Quaich for the next sixteen years with 12 wins between them. I. McCuaig in 1953, '56 and '63, J. MacFarlane in '59, '61, '66 and '68 and A. MacKenzie in '55, '57, '58, '60 and '64. If the original conditions for the trophy had still existed the Quaich would have been MacKenzie's in 1958 after his third win, but the records are of course incomplete. If you thought 5 wins was good how about the seven wins by John MacIntyre senior between 1967 and 1981? This statement must be qualified, however, as there were two different trophies over this period due to the tragic theft of the original Mackie Quaich along with the other trophies in 1968, as previously mentioned. A replacement was donated by White Horse Distillers Ltd. in 1970 and it is now known as the White Horse Trophy. It is not unreasonable to consider the competition as still the original one. It is a pity it did not retain the same name.

The origin of the name White Horse is interesting. Apparently it was the name of an inn at Canongate, Edinburgh, which belonged to the Mackie family. It was in turn named after the white palfrey which carried Mary Queen of Scots to and from the nearby Palace of Holyroodhouse. Which brings us back to golf again as she was reckoned to be one of Scotland's earliest recorded lady golfers. Her notoriety in the golfing sense, came from her reputed devotion to the game. At her trial in London she was accused of playing golf at Seton after having received news of the death of her husband Darnley.

Sir Peter J. Mackie left legacies in many fields, the greatest of which was his contribution to the Scotch Whisky industry. He pioneered the idea of high quality whisky by maturation and linked to a brand name of which White Horse was reckoned to be the first. It shares its birth with the Islay Golf Club and the Machrie Links, all reckoned to be the best of their kind anywhere. White Horse extra fine blended Scotch whisky still survives today, savoured at 19th holes throughout the world.

CHAPTER TEN

THE MACHRIE LINKS

In accordance with the traditions of golf, the site chosen for the Machrie course was perfect. The natural links land with an abundance of sand dunes and long narrow valleys with lush grass kept short by rabbits and sheep were prominent features at Machrie. An early decision was needed regarding the quality of the course to be laid out, short and easy with few hazards, or long and difficult with hazards. The latter was chosen not surprisingly since something special would be necessary to entice golfers from all 'airts' to sample the delights of the Machrie Links. The first tee and clubhouse were sited at Kintra, the nearest point to Port Ellen from where the bulk of the visitors would come.

Willie Campbell was brought in and produced the tough long course as detailed. By any standards of late 19th century golf it was exceptionally long at over 6,000 yards. Uniquely, there was no bogey (par) three hole below 200 yards which meant that for the vast majority of golfers there was no single-shot hole. The hazards were all natural, huge yawning sand holes, high sand dunes on the line of play both for the drive and the approach shots to greens hidden in the valleys beyond. Off the fairways there was tough long marram grass to be avoided at all cost. The holes were not named at the beginning but the lengths were as follows:-

	Yards			Yards
1.	320		10.	330
2.	250		11.	390
3.	204		12.	400
4.	330		13.	435
5.	330		14.	363
6.	360		15.	382
7.	270		16.	285
8.	430	(750)	17.	375
9.	290	(620)	18.	296

OUT 2784 (3434)   IN 3256   Total: 6040 yards   Scratch = 90
(6690 yards)

The layout was as shown on the Course Plan of 1891.

138

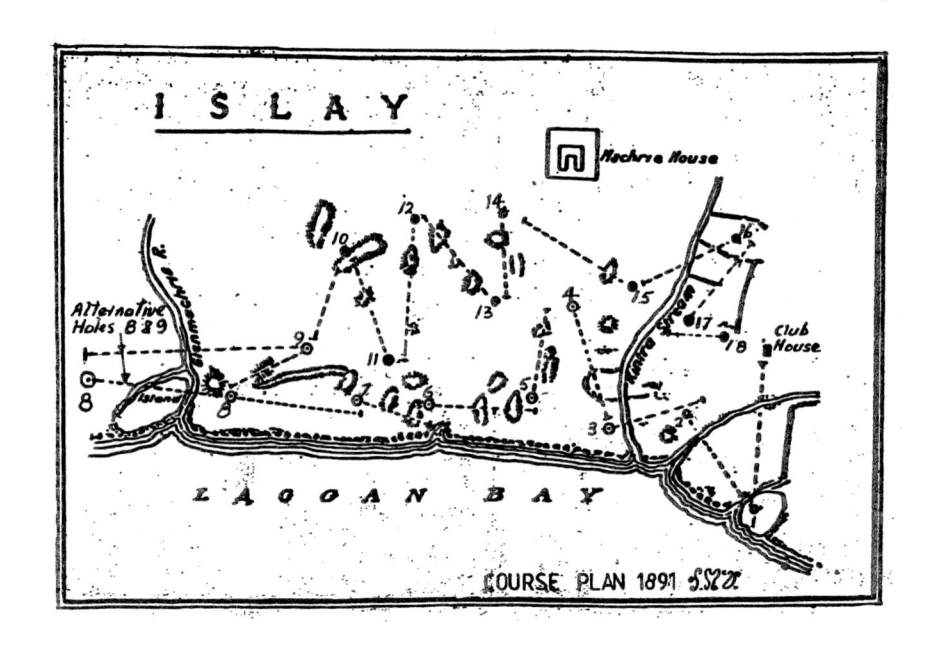

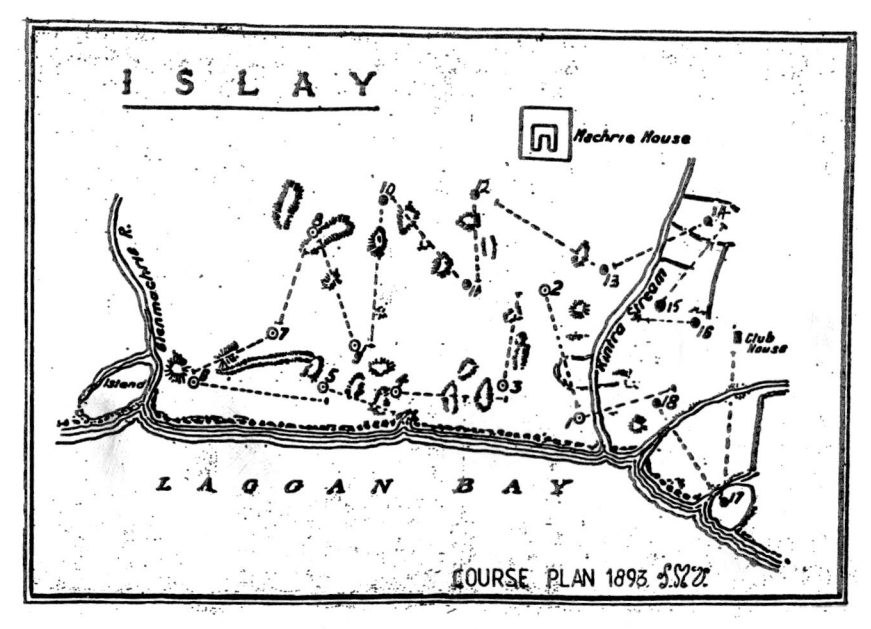

Mount Zion in 1920's.

9th Tee, The Scotman's Maiden early this century.

Not content with having a difficulty factor comparable to the famous links courses at Machrihanish, Prestwick, Troon or Hoylake, two optional holes were provided which increased the length of the course by 650 yards. An optional 8th green was located north of the Glenegedale Burn giving an unbelievable 750 yards hole. The return hole back to the 9th green then became 620 yards long. Not surprisingly these holes just seemed to die a natural death and were not used for the match which opened the course. The bogey score for each hole wasn't fixed at this stage but by comparison with a long hole at Lindrick G.C., also opened in 1891, the bogey score for the 8th hole would have been 8!

The first hole (Mount Zion to be) was proving too difficult as an opening hole. As suggested by the Rev. John Kerr from Dirleton, the order of play was changed so that the round started at Texa (previously hole no 3) thus making Mount Zion hole no 17. This was considered the appropriate position for the most difficult hole of the course, later described by Harry Vardon as the hardest hole he had ever seen. This change was approved by the Committee in August 1893. See layout on Course Plan 1893.

Members and visitors must have been complaining about the lack of a short hole. In April 1894, the 400 yards 10th hole was split into two giving the desired short hole of 158 yards and another of 247 yards. The 15th (Grianan) was eliminated and the 16th re-aligned to suit. The fame of the Islay G.C. and the Machrie Links was spreading rapidly helped by its inclusion in a golf book, *Golfers Guide to Game and Greens of Scotland.* It was published in 1894 and is now a prized collectors' piece. It included a map of the course as reproduced in Course plan 1894 but the lengths of the holes were not stated. However they were included in the Rev. John Kerr's article in the *Golfing Annual* (1893-4, Volume VIII) which also gave the names of the holes and their translation from Gaelic where necessary:

1. TEXA   270 yards
Means 'teaching' because of being adjacent to the derelict site of an old school.

2. CRANNAG   320 yards
Gaelic for pulpit, the hole being placed in an elevated position with a flat area below.

3. LAG   278 yards
Means 'hollow', indicating the position of the putting green.

4. THE SCOTSMAN'S MAIDEN   350 yards
Named after the country's chief newspaper in recognition of its great interest in golf at Islay and the many articles written by Mr.W. Croal, 'one of the most able writers on the game and a frequent visitor to Machrie.'

17th Green between 1901 and 1921

Final of Kildalton Cross in 1935.

5. MANIPUR   268 yards
'Another maiden, but why so named the historian deponeth not. Let us suppose it is to the honour of the gallant lady whose heroism has lately made the name familiar.'

6. GLENEGEDALE   380 yards
Named after adjoining farm. Kerr quotes the Secretary's remarks on the two alternative long holes. 'It would be the occasion of some Bible language being used but it would also give rise to a good deal of fun.'

7. PUNCH BOWL   210 yards
Describes the form of the green. 'Here, as on several other greens, the ridges may be seen that point to days when crofters dwelt in the neighbourhood, and cultivated the hollows, while their 'beasties' grazed on the heights close by.'

8. HEATHER HOLE   295 yards
'So called because of the short heather that covers the ground........it does not interfere much with the lie of the ball, and a good second, with cleek or brassie again brings us to a fine green in another wider hollow, where on a hot day it is very tempting to try some Islay nectar in the shadow of the sloping banks.'

9. WILLIE'S FANCY   320 yards
Thought to be Willie Campbell's favourite hole but Kerr suggests that, pre-golf course days, this was also the area chosen for a putting green by a local worthy named Willie.

10. SHORT HOLE   158 yards
Being the only hole not requiring a wood from the tee Kerr suggests it was nicknamed 'Duffers Delight' before he convinced the club officials to add a bunker in front of the green.

11. DRUIM   247 yards
Means ridge and describes the nature of the ground.

12. IMER   320 yards
Means 'rig and furrow', indicating former cultivation marks on the green - as at Muirfield.

13. MACHRIE   250 yards
'A capital sporting hole reminding us in some respects of the 17th at Prestwick.'

14. AN ABHUINN(An Avon)   375 yards
Named because of its location 'near the river'.

15. GRIANAN   280 yards
Named after a local place.

16. GARADH TOTA   290 yards
'Means 'turf dyke' of which there are three in the hole including one round the putting green. Now opposite the clubhouse, 'we now brace up our courage for the 'pièce de résistance', the noble 17th hole.'

Course Plan 1894

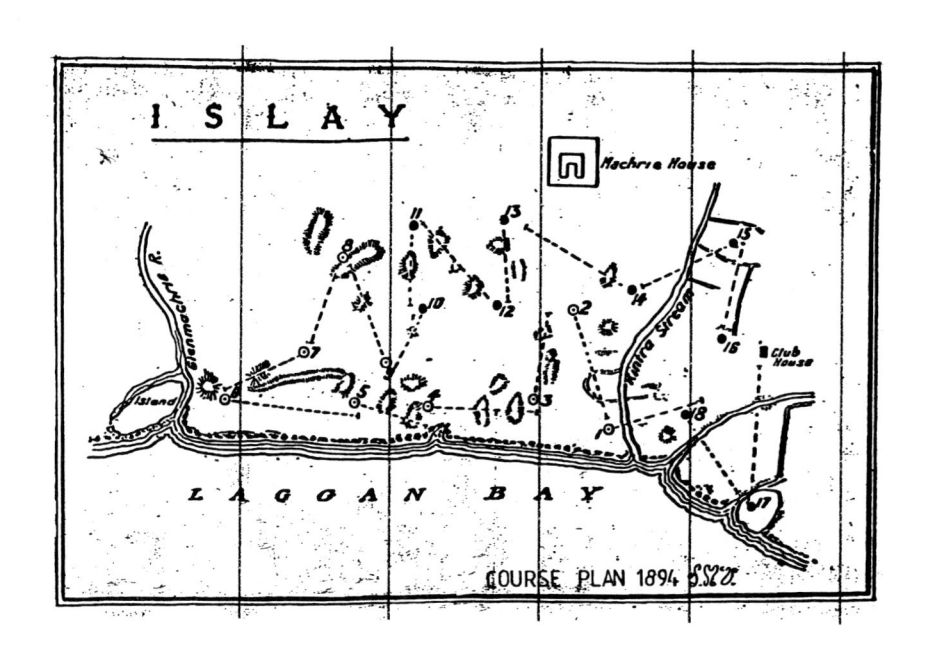

#	Hole	Yards	#	Hole	Yards
1	Texa	270	10	Short Hole	158
2	Crannag	320	11	Druim	247
3	Lag	278	12	Imer	320
4	Scotsman's Maiden	350	13	Machrie	250
5	Manipur	268	14	An Abhuinn	375
6	Glenegedale	380	15	Grianan	280
7	Punch Bowl	210	16	Garadh Tota	290
8	Heather Hole	295	17	Mount Zion	404
9	Willie's Fancy	320	18	The Grave	250
	OUT	2693		IN	2574
				TOTAL	5267

17. KINTRA   404 yards
'Adjacent to Kintra farm but generally called 'Mount Zion' by the locals,..... it is possible to get a 4 at Kintra by a perfect second shot but the player may be quite happy if, after escaping all danger he is safe in the disc after even two more than that.'

18. THE GRAVE   250 yards
An artificial mound on the edge of the green was said to mark the burial place of a number of shipwrecked sailors.

See course plan 1894 for above new layout.

In January 1895, a member, Mr. Mosh from Kendal, urged that the course should be extended into Glenegedale country with the construction of another 6 holes. He sent a donation of £2 towards the costs. The round of 24 holes was given serious consideration as the Committee deliberated for three months after which it just disappeared from the Minutes. One wonders if Mr. Mosh got his money back.

It is no coincidence that in 1895, when Mr.J.S. Higginbotham first joined the Committee, further changes were made to the course. The two short holes, 10 and 11, were reinstated back to a single longer hole and a new 2nd hole, 'Achnamara', was introduced. In addition, no 15, 'Grianan', was taken out and the 16th re-aligned again. A new short hole, 'Imer' was brought in at the expense of shortening 'An Abhuinn'. Thus, two consecutive short holes replaced two similar ones. One wonders why but perhaps the golf wise Mr. Higginbotham had a vision of the future. See course plan 1895.

The original course length of 6040 yards must have been proving too tough for the majority of golfers and in particular the locals. By 1894 the length had been considerably reduced to 5,267 yards, but by the following year it had increased to 5,487 yards.

In 1899, with Higginbotham now Captain, the inevitable happened with the re-arrangement of the course so that the round started and finished at Machrie House, which itself was being extended to cater for the increasing numbers of golfing visitors. These changes were made with thoughts in mind of the forthcoming £100 Islay Tournament. A proposal to redirect the burn beyond Glenegedale to create a new short hole was considered, at the expense of the 18th 'Imer', but no action was taken.

By the construction of new tees and possibly some re-alignment the total length had increased to 5666 yards for the £100 Islay Tournament in 1901. The major change was the extra 100 yards or so added to An Avon (was An Abhuinn), now the first hole. See Course Plan 1901.

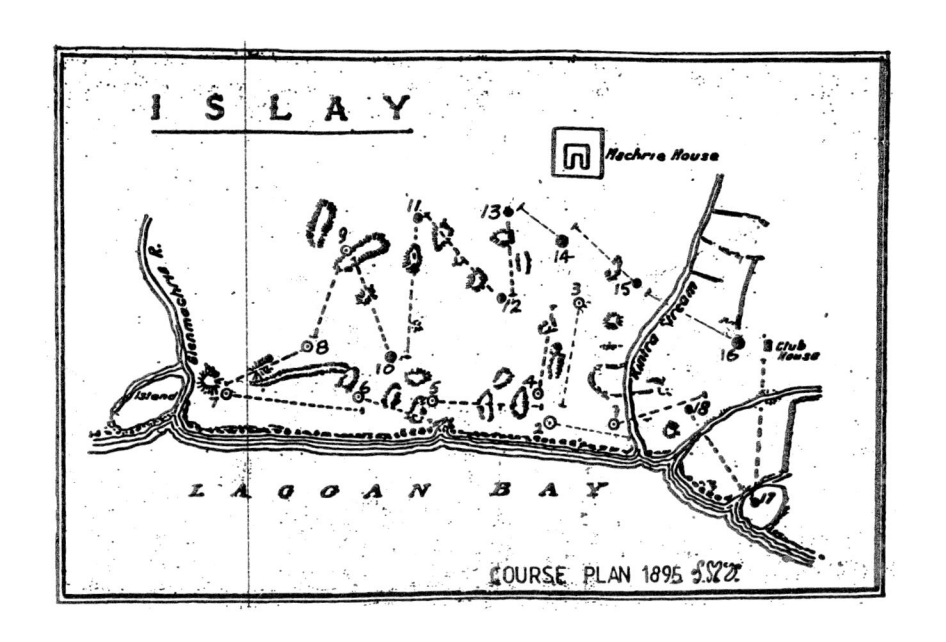

Course Plan 1895

		Yards			Yards
1	Texa	264	10	Willie's Fancy	325
2	Achnamara	338	11	Druim	375
3	Crannag	325	12	Ifrinn	354
4	Lag	270	13	Machrie	365
5	Scotsman's Maiden	360	14	Imer	177
6	Manipur	270	15	An Avon	186
7	Glenegedale	360	16	Gara Tota	348
8	Punch Bowl	205	17	Mount Zion	405
9	Heather Hole	300	18	The Grave	260
	OUT	2692		IN	2795
				TOTAL	5487

The introduction of the revolutionary far flying 'Haskell' rubber cored ball to Britain in 1902 resulted in many courses becoming obsolete due to their lack of distance. Much to the disgust of the traditionalists the lengthening of courses throughout the country was quickly started. There was no immediate similar response by the Islay G.C. possibly due to its natural difficulties. The course had now reached a level of stability which suggested that the best possible layout had finally been achieved after much tinkering with it over its first 10 years. By 1921 the total course length had only increased to 5750 yards. When the S.G.U. fixe ! the scratch score of 76 in 1922 some members wanted the course lengthened to get it back up to 78 but no action was taken. The 177 yard long 18th 'Imer' had not been very popular over the years. At the A.G.M. in 1923 there was much discussion about consulting the legendary James Braid with a view to providing one or two new short holes on the course. It is not clear if Braid was actually consulted but a new 163 yard 8th hole called 'Cruachan' was constructed to replace 'Imer'. It also met with much criticism at the following A.G.M. with the result that the Captain, J.T. MacFarlane, commissioned a report on the course from the professional McAndrew. In spite of a special sub-Committee being formed to discuss his proposals, it was 1927 before only a few minor alterations were agreed. These included the addition of bunkers to 'Cruachan'. The critics had been silenced although a few years later the name was changed to 'Laird's Ain'. The course now measured 5949 yards. See Course Plan 1923.

There were few, if any, even minor changes to the course during the 1930s nor the 1940s and 1950s when survival was the main topic for discussion. It was 1960 before some minor changes occurred. A new tee at Laird's Ain was formed and the front tee of 'Punch Bowl' became the medal tee because it was considered to be too long for a par 3 at 236 yards, but it was later moved back again. New tees also had to be cut at the 6th, 7th and 13th holes, some, because of vandalism by the cattle!

A proposal was put to the A.G.M. in 1962 to do away with the hidden holes on the back nine. It was successfully opposed by Dr. Soutter who claimed that 'Machrie was unique and should be left as it is'. He did promise to look into the possibility and reported back at the next A.G.M. when it was agreed to take no further action. During the 1960s, the Club was unable to obtain other than a year by year lease of the Kintra ground which incorporated holes 2, 3, and 4. Contingency plans were made for the construction of 3 new holes at Glenegedale and these were officially adopted at the A.G.M. in 1969. The historic blind holes were under attack again as the Minutes stated 'no hidden holes'. The proposed new 10th, 11th and 12th holes were cut and maintained initially but by 1971 the failure to maintain these

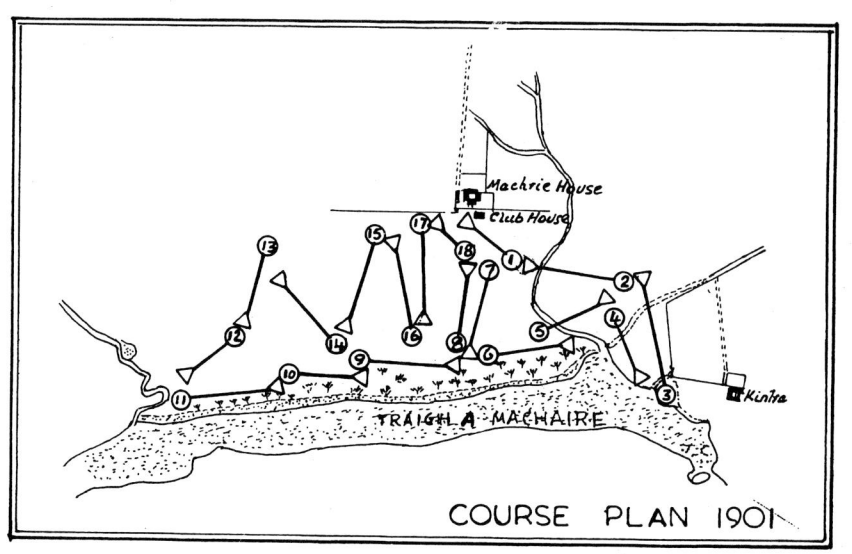

COURSE PLAN 1901

Course Plan 1901

		Yards
1	An Avon	275
2	Gara Tota	348
3	Mount Zion	420
4	The Grave	260
5	Texa	264
6	Achnamara	312
7	Crannag	325
8	Lag	300
9	Scotsman's Maiden	400
	OUT	2904

		Yards
10	Manipur	276
11	Glenegedale	380
12	Punch Bowl	205
13	Heather Hole	300
14	Willie's Fancy	325
15	Druim	375
16	Ifrinn	354
17	Machrie	370
18	Imer	177
	IN	2762
	TOTAL	5666

Bogey(1921) = 80
Bogey(1922) = 76

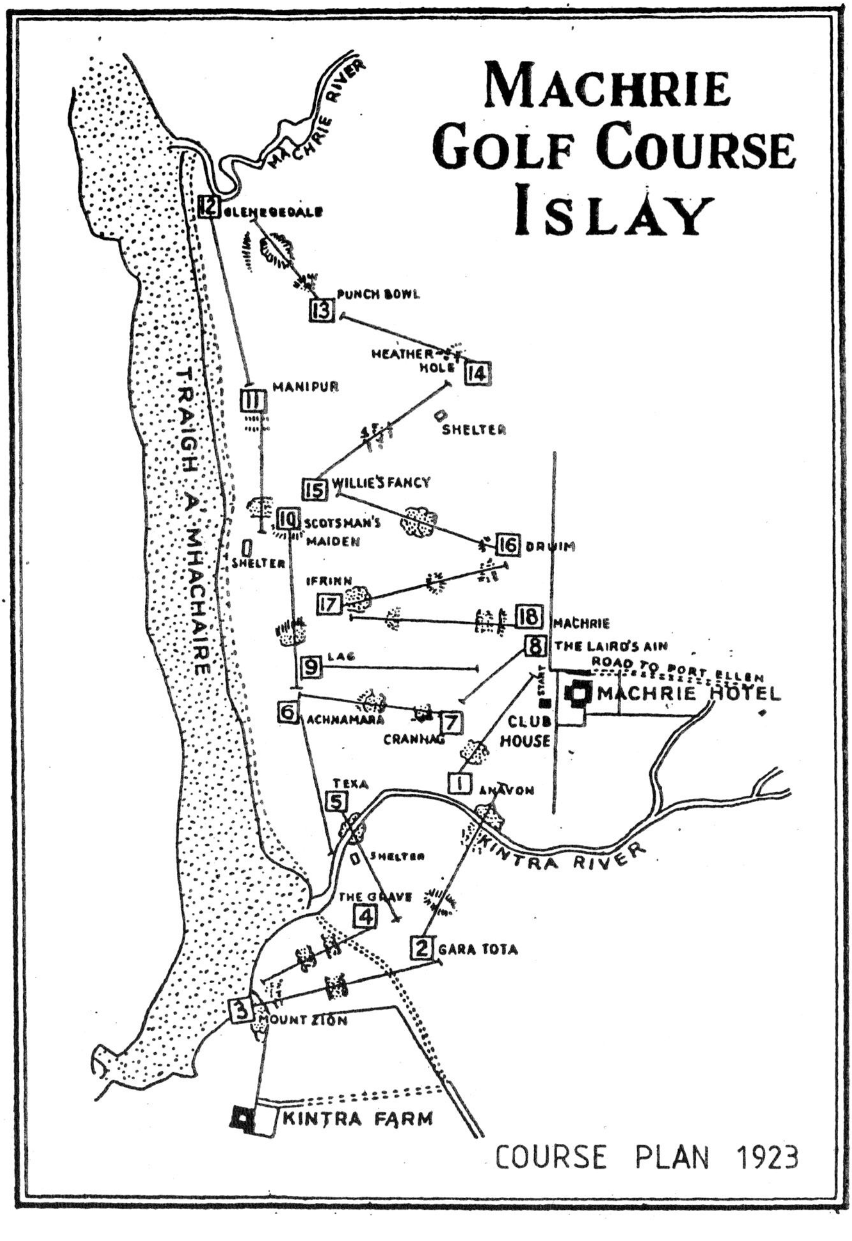
MACHRIE
GOLF COURSE
ISLAY
MACHRIE RIVER
12 GLENEGEDALE
13 PUNCH BOWL
HEATHER HOLE
14
11 MANIPUR
SHELTER
15 WILLIE'S FANCY
10 SCOTSMAN'S MAIDEN
16 DRUIM
SHELTER
IFRINN
17
18 MACHRIE
8 THE LAIRD'S AIN
ROAD TO PORT ELLEN
9 LAG
START
MACHRIE HOTEL
6 ACHNAMARA
7
CRANNAG
CLUB HOUSE
TRAIGH A' MHACHAIRE
1 ANAVON
TEXA
5
SHELTER
KINTRA RIVER
THE GRAVE
4
2 GARA TOTA
3 MOUNT ZION
KINTRA FARM
COURSE PLAN 1923

holes was attributed to the satisfactory assurances on the continuation of the Kintra lease. Further unsuccessful attempts were made to eliminate the hidden holes but all thoughts of change disappeared with the arrival of new owners, Machrie Developments Ltd. in 1976. This completes the details of the changes to the Links throughout the 85 years when, except for the short period in the 1940s, they were solely under the care of the Islay Golf Club.

The further major improvements to the course by Machrie Developments Ltd. have already been detailed in Chapter 7. In conclusion the final length (6226 yards) was back where it started in 1891 at over 6,000 yards but now with a combination of old and new features which met with enthusiastic approval from all. See Course Plan 1979.

Course Plan 1923

		Yards			Yards
1	An Avon	308	10	Scotsman's Maiden	395
2	Gara Tota	372	11	Manipur	320
3	Mount Zion	425	12	Glenegedale	392
4	The Grave	264	13	Punchbowl	236
5	Texa	270	14	Heather Hole	341
6	Achnamara	320	15	Willie's Fancy	335
7	Crannag	343	16	Druim	396
8	Cruachan	163	17	Ifrinn	352
9	Lag	343	18	Machrie	374
	OUT	2808		IN	3141
				TOTAL	5949
				Bogey(1930)	= 74

N.B. Cruachan changed to Laird's Ain pre-1936

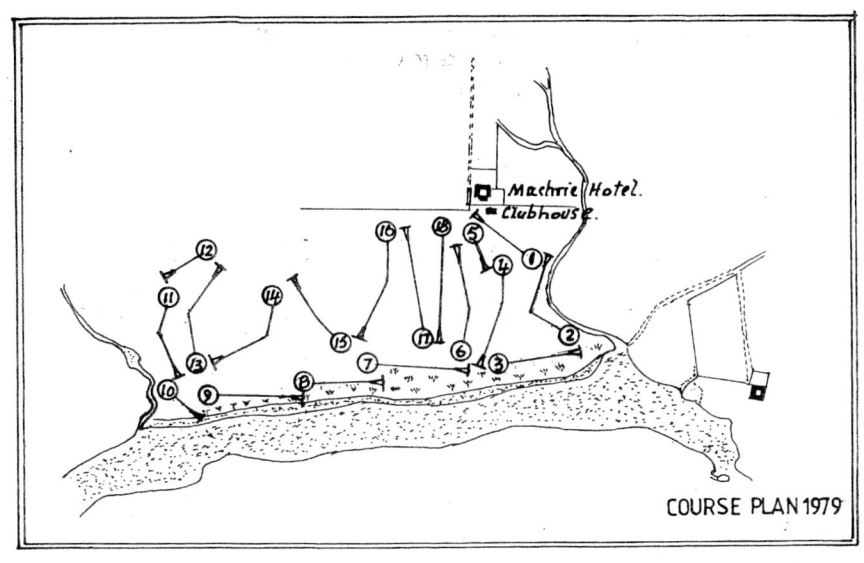

COURSE PLAN 1979

Course Plan 1979

		Yards	Par
1	An Avon	308	4
2	Kintra	508	5
3	Achnamara	319	4
4	Crannag	390	4
5	Lairds' Ain	163	3
6	Lag	344	4
7	Scotsman's Maiden	395	4
8	Manipur	337	4
9	Glenegedale	392	4
	OUT	3156	36
10	Machrie Burn	156	3
11	The Skor	357	4
12	New Mount Zion	174	3
13	Lochindaal	488	5
14	Heather Hole	423	4
15	Willie's Fancy	335	4
16	Druim	411	4
17	Ifrinn	352	4
18	Machrie	374	4
	IN	3070	35
	TOTAL	6226	
	PAR		71
	S.S.S.		70

150

CHAPTER ELEVEN

MEMORIES

Theoretically, the Past Captains should be the ideal source for information on the memorable happenings during their term on Committee. Letters were sent by Tom Dunn to all known P.C.'s asking for a written contribution to the history of the Golf Club. The high quality of the replies compensates for the small number submitted. Some of the longer contributions have with difficulty been curtailed by the author due to space restrictions, not censorship! They have been arranged in chronological order of the year in office so that maturity decided who got in the first Lachie Mackinnon story!

Dr. Alex McCorkindale Campbell D.S.O.,O.B.E.,T.D.,M.B.,CH.B.
Captain 1936-37

Sandwiched between the inaugural Kildalton Challenge Cross competition and the famous £100 Islay Tournament was the birth of Alex(Lex) Campbell at Ardbeg, Islay in 1901. Ninety-two years later while on holiday he was invited to attend the dinner during Cross week when he was made an Honorary Member. Unbelievably this sprightly nonagenarian submitted his golfing memories in very clear handwriting, remarkable for any doctor of any age!

After attending Ardbeg primary school and Hillhead High School in Glasgow, he studied medicine at Glasgow University where he graduated in 1925. He returned to Islay via South Wales, to be Medical Officer for the Parish of Kildalton and Oa in April 1928. This appointment came 3 weeks after he was turned down because at 26 he was too young and knew too many people in the area. He married the following year and remained on Islay until called up in 1939 for war service. Lex now lives in Skipton, Yorkshire, with his daughter but hopes to spend more time in future at the family home in Port Ellen. He writes of his golfing memories at Machrie.

1929/30. The Captain, Dr. Chadborn, with "Cross" finalists and caddies.

"Cross" Presentation of 1937 with Dr. A. M. Campbell the Captain standing in centre.

'During my time working in Islay I played golf regularly at Machrie. I played mainly in a foursome in which were two older members and a younger one much about my own age. ..... We two younger ones often snatched a game by ourselves. About the mid-thirties a

Dr. Alex McC. Campbell (Captain 1936-37) with the "Cross" in 1993.

new minister came to the area, a comparatively young man. One day he asked if he might join us at Machrie and we said, "Of course by all means," but we regretted our readiness to accept him as a golfing partner - we discovered that he had never played before and he was painfully slow. He took 12 'wiggles' in addressing the ball and often missed it completely and had to go through the whole procedure again! I remember one occasion, approaching the 11th green - his ball was on an upward slope and he took aim as usual, gave a terrific swipe, and fell on his back and rolled down the slope. We really began to feel that we would have to tell him to stop; but he was such a nice chap that we hadn't the heart to do anything about it. Fortunately for us he himself realized soon after that golf wasn't for him and he gave it up.

On another occasion all four of us carried on for the full round and at the 10th tee every one of us drove right into the Maiden bunker. There was a young chap (a holiday visitor) sitting at the top of the bunker and as we toiled up the slope after eventually getting our balls out one of our number spoke to the visitor and said, "its a sair fecht." "Aye," he said, "are you all beginners?"

Alex refers to an incident in the Western Isles Open Championship in 1935 involving the professional, Archie Compston, whom he described as 'a rather course loud-mouthed sort of individual':

'I happened to be among a group of spectators at the 13th hole when he was about to play it and there happened to be a clergyman spectator. Compston looked round and shouted in a loud voice, "How the hell do you expect me to play this hole when there's a bloody priest about!" '

Perhaps Alex's nice chap thinking of taking up the game again!.
He continued:

'I was never much good as a player myself but I was extremely enthusiastic and fond of the game. I did on two occasions get a hole in one at the short 8th, but that was a mere fluke I'm sure.'

We look forward to his presence at the Kildalton Cross Centenary in the year 2000!

Alexander Gray M.A. L.L.B.
Captain 1953-54

'I regret that my period of office was so long ago that I recollect little of it..... I first joined the club about 1925 as a junior. The membership fee was then 15 shillings. At that time there were two greenkeepers - John MacMillan, who had been a professional in his day and Willie Whyte. John was much older than Willie and had ceased to golf at that time but Willie (who wore a special boot and ankle attachment as a result of a war wound) could go round the course in a steady 72 and was much in demand for 'bounce' games with Hotel residents after his day on the greens.

The greens in those days were cut with heavy handmowers. Each greenkeeper cut four greens daily. As boys we used to take turns of pushing these mowers and found it very hard work indeed. The fairways were cut by a large barrel mower drawn by horse and shafted rather like an ordinary farm-cart. In the late autumn the greenkeepers lay out on straw pallets on the greens and extracted the daisies with small handforks.

I remember being told that in the early days of the development of the golf ball (was it the 'Haskell'?) John McMillan took part in a professional competition of the time. The top prize was £100 and the round had to be completed using the same ball. John was leading at the 17th when his ball disintegrated.

In the 1920s the greenkeepers had a small hut adjoining the first tee. Club repairs were undertaken and golf balls etc. could be purchased. In school holiday periods there was a daily supply of caddies from Port Ellen and bookings were arranged by the greenkeepers.

Recently when the three new holes were taken in it was intriguing to learn of the large amount of adders which were found. I myself killed one on the 13th tee. What brings the matter to mind is that I recollect John McMmillan telling me one day that he had killed an adder on Druim green and that that was the first one he had ever encountered on the course over the many years he had worked there.'

Mr. Gray doesn't remember much happening during his year as Captain which is not surprising as it was a very quiet year. However he can lay claim to being a substitute for a Walker Cup golfer, but not because of his golfing prowess. He willingly accepted the honour of being Captain in place of Vice-Captain, Roy C. MacGregor, who postponed his nomination for a year due to his participation in the Walker Cup. The Islay GC at this time was just recovering from near oblivion at the end of the war. It is obvious that during Mr. Gray's Captaincy he ensured that full attention was paid to maintaining the course. On his election as Captain, Roy stated, that the course was as near perfect as he had ever seen it. Not too many retiring Captains can claim to have had such praise from such an authoritative source.

Robert H. Gibb
Captain 1963-64

Although Mr.Gibb was not on the current membership list he was successfully tracked down by Tom Dunn. His excellent contribution covers three decades of golf on Islay and epitomises the magic of Islay, its golf course and its people. His comments and notes on his year of Captaincy are as follows:

A.G.M. - Manny Ayres and his Balance sheet - piece of old wallpaper. Details handwritten - approved.

Matt Armstrong complained that the hole at Achnamara had moved 6" whilst he was putting. Pointed out to him that it was perhaps the night before that had been the cause.

John Morrison and John MacIntyre Senior all square after 18 holes. I, being Captain, was asked for a ruling as to what now happened. There had been considerable discussion at the A.G.M. - whether the best of the first 3 holes with strokes, or without strokes.

Anyway, I gave my decision, and off they set. John Morrison won at Mount Zion. When they returned to the Hotel, they disappeared into the bar. However, someone pointed out to me that I had given the wrong decision. Ralph Middleton, the then secretary, was contacted on the 'phone and asked to look up his Minutes. Some 40 Minutes had elapsed when he informed me that I had been wrong - the match was ALL SQUARE. I had the dubious pleasure of informing the two contestants that they had to go all the way to Mount Zion and continue playing. John MacIntyre won at the Grave. Both contestants took it all in the finest spirit. This could only happen in Islay.!

That year, Dugie McKinnon and John MacIntyre contested the final and I was required to referee. Dugie was 5 up after the first 18 holes. The afternoon round was witnessed by a goodly crowd, plus Bert Marshall. On the 1st tee, Dugie had the honour. He tee'd up his ball slightly in front of the marker, but before I had time to say anything, Bert did. "Dugie, you teed oop six inches in't front of bloody marker." Dugie proceeded to hook his ball out of bounds into the field. Needless to say, he lost the first 5 holes.

They arrived at the 36th hole all square. John was short of the green and in an impossible lie. Someone said, "that's a rabbit scrape." I never said a word - John looked me straight in the eye - he never said a word, and attempted to play the shot. He failed - it was impossible - and he lost winning the Cross by 1 hole. That epitomised the spirit of golf on Islay.

I will always be eternally grateful to the Islay Golf Club for appointing me as their Captain. I will look back on 'the good old days' with many happy memories.'

Mr. Gibb's year was not without incident. At the A.G.M., after lengthy discussions on the procedure after a tie in the Cross after 18 holes, a motion was approved for sudden death thereafter, without handicap allowance. This explains the revised ruling above. Other Cross decisions were confirmation of the maximum handicap as 12, the defeat of a motion for seeding and the elimination of the need to qualify which was referred to the Committee. A previous Committee decision to have G.U.R. at Mount Zion was rescinded at the A.G.M. which possibly explains a friendly contra-temps the author had at this hole not long afterwards in a bounce game with Tim Morrison. It was my first ever game at Machrie and rabbit scrape or G.U.R on the fringe at the back of the green at Mount Zion was the point under discussion, before I gave in, played the ball as it lay and got a half. Coming off the 8th green I was a few holes up when a black cloud and a few spots of rain appeared. We headed for the clubhouse and a drink to find a ceilidh in full swing. That was the end of the golf match!'

Mr. Gibb continued his contribution with some memorable incidents from his many years visiting Islay and incidentally, also included the first version of the Lachie Mackinnon story.

Memorabilia of Machrie and the Islay Golf Club.

' It was 1955 when I paid my first visit to Machrie. An old family friend by the name of Mrs. T. H. Crerar suggested I should go. She and her husband were regular visitors to Machrie in the late 30s. There was, she said, a very good golf competition called 'The Kildalton Cross' held every year in August.

So a very good friend, Murray McCash, and myself, booked a two week's stay with Bert Marshall. The first experience of the golf course was a bit of an adventure. We negotiated the first ten holes without too much difficulty. Having driven off Manipur tee, we were somewhat perplexed. There was only one green to be seen. A funny sort of hole this, we said. An adjacent tee did have a modicum of a tee box which said 'No. 16'. We had in fact played onto the 15th green (Willie's fancy).

After some exploring, we found the proper green. Glenegedale was reasonably straightforward. Then we were lost. No sign of a tee - certainly no sign of a green. Again after much exploring, we discovered Punch Bowl green. Heather hole was not too difficult - nor was Willie's fancy. Druim posed a few problems, but when we came to Ifrinn we were lost again. In the end, after much exploratory work, we found the green - and then Machrie. We were home at last, after some 4 hours and a bit. Gradually we got to know the course, and to love it.

That year, 1955, Murray and I shared the bungalow with Forrest Anderson and Bill Brownlie. Apart from the occasional visit from a cow, we had the place to ourselves.

In the first round of the Cross, I met Billy Kerr - a licensed grocer from Glasgow. Two holes of a start I had to concede. Well, I could drive the ball and I could putt, but anything with an iron blade was the awful- dare I say it- SHANK! The first hole, having played 5 shots, I was somewhere on the banks of the Garatota burn. The 2nd - similar result- heading towards the beach. So it went on until I reached the Maiden (the old 10th)

Roy MacGregor had been watching me through a pair of binoculars. "What on earth are you doing?" he said, and when I told him he replied, "I shouldn't give advice, but don't address the ball, select the club, walk up to it, and hit it." Gilbert Stevenson was caddying for me, and he must have wondered what he had been lumbered with. Well, I took Roy's advice, got a birdie 3 at the Maiden and another one at Manipur. Billy went over the fence at Glenegedale, out of bounds, and when we arrived at Machrie tee, I was dormie one up. I won the last hole and finished two up - a memorable game of golf, indeed it was.

Beginners luck, that year 1955, I went on to the final, to be beaten 3 and 2 by Dr Iain Henderson of Renfrew. 1956 and '57 I went back to Machrie, missed '58 and '59, then returned in 1960. The 60s have many memories. The highlight was of course, 1964 when I won the Cross. My old buddy Murray McCash was the opponent and I managed to win by one hole. I will always remember the 36th hole. John MacIntyre was my caddy and he handed me my spoon on the tee. "Get the first shot to the green," he said. That was when I hit the best shot of my life - a no 5 iron onto the right side of the green, pin high. That was enough. Another high point was 1971 when I managed to win the Club Championship. 72 was my second round - one of the best I've ever managed over Machrie.

Dr. McCash and his wife used to potter onto the course for a few holes. One day they appeared back at the Hotel, Mrs. McCash looking like a drowned rat. "'My husband" she said, "pushed me into the burn - would you believe it?" What had happened was that one of their golf balls had ended up in the burn in front of the then Texa green. Dr. McCash didn't feel he could reach it, so Mrs. McCash volunteered to lie down on the ground and try to fetch it out with a golf club. She got to the point of no-return, and the Doctor, being unwilling to try to pull her back, decided to push her into the burn. From that day on she was known as Mrs. McSplash.

We all spent our summer holidays at Machrie and the children loved it. No 2 son was very young and had high tea. His mother and I took turns at dinner time to go and listen to make sure he had settled. Usually he was a bit restive for the first few nights, but on this occasion there wasn't a sound from the bedroom. Eventually we peeked into the room - there was Russell fast asleep in his cot immersed in a pile of wallpaper which he had carefully and meticulously peeled off the wall. The next year we had the same rooms. The wallpaper had been patched but not with a matching wallpaper - something totally different in colour and pattern. Bert hadn't minded. "You know what kids are like," he said.

One of my vivid memories was of the water supply. Regularly the tanks dried up, and there would be one loo working in the whole hotel. If you wanted a bath it was either the burn or the sea.

I remember, too the 'one club to Mount Zion', after dinner on a balmy evening. Everybody turned out, young and old, and Malcolm McNeil would be there at Mount

Zion green with his bags of sweeties. Talking of Mount Zion, and of course Kintra, Archie McNeill used to always have a caravan there for his holiday. One night, Lachie Mackinnon decided to go and visit Archie - on foot, over the golf course. He had gone via Texa and of course had to cross the burn. 'Well," said Lachie, "I was always pretty good at the long jump when I was at school." Unfortunately, he said he got into the 'stall' position - the rest can be imagined.

Memories of Duncan MacCalman scything the bracken at the last hole because he could drive into it, and of Dougie McDougall playing with me in a match, visitors v locals. I had lost my ball at Heather hole and, having found the ball, informed the rest. Dougie was still searching through the rough and when I said, "It's all right Dougie, I've found it," he replied, "It's not your ball I'm looking for. I've lost my 'bludy' clubs."

Memories of Bert's bumpy road, as we call it. In any weather, you could see someone coming from the moment they turned at the Machrie road end. A cloud of dust signified that your golfing partner or opponent was due to arrive in a minute.

All my memories are connected with games of golf and conviviality in the bar afterwards with some of the finest people I have been privileged to know. The Mackinnons, Alan MacKenzie, John Morrison, Gilbert Johnson, Gilbert Stevenson, Forrest Anderson, Bill Brownlie, the Soutters, John MacIntyre senior and junior, the McNeils, the Russells, Ian McCuaig, John Campbell, Manny Ayres, Ralph Middleton, the Simes, - the list is endless.'

John A. Mason C.A.
Captain 1977-8

When John Mason stepped up to the hot seat on 1st August 1977 after Vice-Captain, Eliot Soutter, had declined the Captaincy, the Club was still in the throes of coming to terms with the arrival of the new owners of the hotel and course, Machrie Developments Ltd. (Bowmore Holdings). They had money to spend on improvements and thus began an exciting era for Islay golfers which was to see the full potential of the hotel and golf course being developed to their highest ever standard. John shares some memories of his Captaincy :

' I was Captain of Islay Golf Club during 1977/78 and during my year of office the only noteworthy event was the drafting of a Club Constitution. This Constitution was agreed by members at the A.G.M. in August 1978.

The Hotel and Golf Course had recently changed over to the control of Bowmore Holdings and Tim Morrison was a Committee member throughout 1977/78 and assisted greatly with the drafting of the new Constitution.

Also during my year of office two golf weeks were held under the eagle eye of David Huish. These golf weeks were sponsored by Mid-Argyll Tourist Board of which Lachie MacKinnon was an integral part.

Lachie Mackinnon was a distinguished war pilot who was born and bred on Islay. During the summer of 1977 he had partaken of some typical Island hospitality and he decided to play the first eight holes. (In those days of the old course). When Lachie reached the 5th hole, known as Texa, he played his second shot onto the green. To avoid the long detour to the bridge over the burn, Lachie decided to have a run and jump over the burn.

In Lachies own words, "half way across the burn I found myself in the stall position." Lachie decided to dry off, lying in the dunes and he carefully pierced his pound notes on the bents. Lachie dozed off and when he awoke he saw his pound notes blowing along the 6th fairway. In hot pursuit, Lachie eventually ingathered his money just before reaching the 'Maiden'.'

Only one noteworthy event? As far as the author is concerned there was one other - the introduction for the first time of typed reports which eliminated the time consuming guessing game when trying to decypher some of the handwritten reports of the previous 86 years. Other nearly noteworthy events were the retiral of Hon. Secretary, J. McGregor, to be replaced by Douglas Stone, unsuccessful attempts to get ladies on the Committee, concern about high sums of money at stake in the auction, entrance fee re-introduced, new set of local rules and the formation of a Ladies Liason sub-Committee.

W. Douglas Calder
Captain 1983-84

Douglas Calder was the principal contributor to the writing of the new Constitution in 1977-78. When he was elected Captain in August 1983 the 'Morrison Era' had just ended. The Golf Club was in a healthy position and the golf course in excellent condiiton. The Constitution had to be altered to allow members the choice of membership by paying the appropriate annual fee or the weekly/fortnightly fees at Cross time. Douglas Calder produced another Lachie MacKinnon story.

' My own contribution for consideration among material to be used in the book is a favourite incident during the year I was Captain of the Club. In the Club Championship the late Lachie Mackinnon was partnered with 'Puda' Brown. Before they started their round 'Puda' marked the first 5 holes on Lachie's card 4,5,3,5,1. Lachie then proceeded to play the first 5 holes exactly as 'Puda' had marked including the hole in one at Laird's Ain. I cannot recollect whether they went on to finish the round or turned sharp right into the Hotel bar!'

Sadly, seven months after submiting his contribution, Douglas was drowned in Loch Lomond and didn't get the chance to participate in the Centenary celebrations.

Robin C. MacGregor
Captain 1985-86

Not many golfers can lay claim to a father (Roy C. MacGregor) who was a Scottish Internationalist and Walker Cup player. Robin didn't match his father's golfing achievements but he had the unique honour of following in his father's footsteps as a Captain. Robin wrote:

' We had many happy holidays at Machrie from 1950-1957 with a break in 1953 when father was playing with the Walker Cup team in America. My favourite incident on the course was at Anavon tee (the 1st). Matt Armstrong was playing with Melville Lang, my father and another. He had bought some new clubs and the woods were very small headed. He always used a high tee and after a practice swing he drove. Unfortunately he went clean under the ball, nicking it slightly. The ball rose up almost in slow motion and hit him on the head. Melville Lang in monotone voice, 'playing four'.

In 1965 Innes McMaster and myself arrived on Islay in my Morris Minor 1000 saloon prospecting for camp sites. We stayed at David Mottram's hotel, the 'Sea View' I think. When David heard we were going to play in the 'Cross', he suggested dinner bed and breakfast with him for 21/- or was it 27/6. Our sleeping accommodation was in our sleeping bags on top of old bed frames in the old Post Office in Shore Street (which David Mottram owned). We lunched at Machrie and had sometimes three helpings of each course. Bert Marshall was very hospitable. We stayed at Machrie the next year, 5 boys to a room for £18 full board, second and third helpings of every course!

There were lots of friends and friendly foes like Lachie and Dougie Mackinnon who played a bounce game against Bob Gibb and myself the morning after I had got engaged at 5.10am. Bob and I won at the 13th, Punch Bowl. The two Mackinnons weren't satisfied and we played byes to the 23rd hole where our winnings had dropped to 10p. Whereupon we retired to the bar and were informed that the winners buy the drinks! There's hope for us all yet - John MacFarlane won the 'Cross' when he was 65?66!!

My year as Captain, 1985-86 was great fun. I was knocked out in the second round and felt quite relieved! As John MacIntyre said, "It gives you time to concentrate on the organisation of the week and the dinner". I had managed 6 visits during the year and 6 the previous year, all meetings to take place when there was a Medal! I remember before the 2nd round of the final I had to drive myself in and was suitably refreshed by friends with several Gins and Cinzanos. I walked onto the tee and hit the longest and straightest drive of my life, wearing ordinary shoes and being quite relaxed.

The A.G.M. went well that year. Friends of the Earth, David Bellamy et al plus the argumentative types all went to a meeting in Bowmore about geese. The quickest and quietest meeting ever!

After Bert sold Machrie to Alastair Gray and Melville Lang (my uncle), the facilities started to improve and by the time the Morrisons of Bowmore had bought Machrie the Hotel was going more up market. With a short season and heavier investment where there was none before, the character of the hotel changed. Gone were the days of DIY where Bert and his daughters and wife Enid did the decorating and the Golf Club locals kept the course for next to nothing. The new owners and finally Murdo MacPherson spent a lot on the hotel and course. Two very different ways of doing things and hard to reconcile the two without friction at the interface!'

Robin continues wth his summary of the magic of Islay ;

'A place I find relaxing, fun, hospitable and a place I want to be when I am not thinking of it, when I am, I feel at peace. A place where you can enjoy a game of golf so much you forget about winning and just delight in being there. Only one other place in the world like it with a manyana sort of feel to it, Corfu,where they speak Greek instead of Gaelic and the weather is warmer, not necessarily better.'

Max McGill
Captain 1987-88

It was inevitable that Max, a devotee of Islay golf since being first introduced to 'Cross' week by Robin MacGregor in the 60s, should follow closely on his heels as Captain. He writes:-

'Having travelled to Islay for over 20 years and being conscious of the considerable traditions of the club I have always felt that there was something special to being a Member of the Islay Golf Club. It was with particular pleasure and pride that I was elected Vice-Captain of the Club in 1986 and Captain the following year.

The highlight of any Captain's year in Islay has to be 'Cross Week' and it was a week which demanded intense effort but one which I thoroughly enjoyed. Of the many incidents in a packed week two things stand out in my memory. On the Thursday night in the absence of my Vice Captain, Gilbert Stevenson, John Calder my predecessor as Captain, readily agreed, over a glass or two, to referee the first round of the final the following morning. I awoke the next day to find it teeming with rain. Rather than enjoy a lie I got up and went over to the first tee to find out if John was still as enthusiastic about the task as he had been in the early hours of the morning. He was still determined to see it through, his only concern being that he lost his wallet the previous night. After a long walk round the golf course in the rain he was relieved to find that his wallet was still in his jacket pocket where he had left it the night before!

The weather cleared at lunch time on the same day and the rain almost ceased as I drove into office immediately prior to the second round of the final. As the ritual shotgun was not in evidence I was not subjected to any interruption and contrived to hit two of my best drives of the week. The second, for a bottle of whisky, struck a well kent supporter hard and high on the left thigh but he valiantly hirpled back to the tee to claim his prize. I suppose I should not have been surprised to find that the bottle was already finished after 5 holes of a well fought local final.'

Gilbert Stevenson
Captain 1988-89

Undoubtedly the furthest travelled Past Captain's contribution was that of Gilbert Stevenson, from Dhahran, Saudi Arabia:

'As Monty had found the Western Desert to be an ideal place for developing strategies, I decided to spend my year as Vice Captain in Benghazi, with frequent visits to Islay, to plan my strategy when Captain of Islay Golf Club in 1988. I can't say that ultimately I was as successful as Monty, but then he had only to contend with Rommel and the Africa Korps!

Kildalton Cross Week, the highlight of the year, was very successful. The course was immaculate, the weather good and the ozone laden atmosphere, as always, a joy to savour. Thanks to the motivating skills of Alistair McLachlan, auctioneer, and the generosity of members, Cross Auction proceeds amounted to a record £3,109.

Mrs. Audrey MacCalman (widow of the late Duncan MacCalman) made the draw for the Kildalton Cross and the Kildalton Plate competitions. The Kildalton Cross, with 86 entrants, was keenly contested. Roddie MacGregor beat John McKean in a quality final. The afternoon round of the final went to Ifrinn (Hell-in Gaelic). Derek Gray won the Club Championship. Frazer Irvine lifted the Kildalton Plate. Prizes were presented by my wife Sheena. I didn't win anything!

The Kildalton Cross dinner was as usual, a sell-out and guest speakers were Elaine Samuel, Ian Muir and John Calder. They gave very spirited performances to an equally spirited audience. In retrospect, it was a typical hot Islay night and we started toasting (in every sense) prematurely. I should have deferred the toasts until the desserts had been served and devoured thereby obviating the need for straws in place of cutlery.

Being a local Captain, I was of the opinion that mainland members, who constituted around 50 per cent of the total membership, would welcome being informed of routine and special Islay Golf Club business. Consequently, the Islay Golf Club Newsletter was introduced and the feedback from members was more than positive.

The support provided to me by my Vice-Captain (Tom Irvine), the immediate Past Captain (Max McGill), the Ladies Section (Captain Margaret Hastie), the Committee and Islay Golf Club members coupled with the extraordinary efforts of Dianne and Alex Brown and Tim Morrison, on behalf of the Junior Section, were very inspiring. The efforts and dedication of Islay Golf Club members (both known and unknown to me) of yesteryear were also a major inspiration.

It is personally gratifying to be participating in Islay Golf Club's Centenary Celebrations and I am optimistic that Islay Golf Club shall endure and celebrate its Bicentenary. The honour and pride which I experienced through being Captain of Islay Golf Club shall certainly endure in my time. '

Alastair Shanks

The final contribution in this chapter comes from one who was neither a Past Captain or even a member of the Islay Golf Club. It was submitted by the late Alastair Shanks and apart from its historical aspect it represents the many local and visiting golfers who over the years have enjoyed golf on the Machrie Links without feeling the need to join the competitive card and pencil corps of a golf club. Alastair had the interests of the Golf Club at heart and in times of need gave frequent anonymous donations to the Club. His typed contribution came from his home in Port Ellen in response to an appeal from Murdo MacPherson for historical information on Islay golf:

' My information is mostly second-hand as I was brought up in Glasgow and came here only on holidays in the early days and I am now 80 years old, but I pass on such things as I remember hearing from my father and from my aunts (who lived here all their days) but please check if you can as I know such handed-on information can be very unreliable.

First you ask about Ronald McArthur. I remember him being referred to as 'the Artist' and of seeing him, I think in knickerbockers (i.e. plus fours)........ Also I can confirm that he made golf clubs, though my version is that he made a set for Mr. Asquith (not necessarily contradicting the other version). One of my aunts, a teacher in the local school, played golf mainly on the old local course, (on the hill behind Ramsay Hall and over to the old Free Church - called Geisgeire). She had two clubs which she said were made by him and they were in due course inherited by my late brother and myself. They were a mashie and an iron but there was no sign of a design on the back. Perhaps that was only applied to 'special editions', or may have been concealed by years of rust. I gave my one to either the hotel or the club a number of years ago when the bar lunch area had a small display of old clubs on the wall. I do not know what may have happened to it - there was nothing distinctive about it to anyone who did not know the history (which I passed on at the time, but which may not have been passed on when the hotel changed hands). I was told just recently that McArthur was a small stoutish man-but it was a long time ago and I would have been rather young at the time and may be confusing with some other memory.

The remainder is anecdote but may be of interest. I was told (my father played golf at Machrie in his day and more recently my cousin, Dr. Bisset - both collectors of stories) that a match was played between four of the top professionals of the day - the names of Braid, Vardon and Taylor come to mind. One story was that when they came to 'The Maiden' (which was and possibly still is a substantial hillock of sand, fringed with menacing bent grass just at an awkward distance from the tee for the clubs of those days) the first three to tee off failed to clear the height with their drives and landed in the sand. Taylor took his driver and deliberately 'pulled' his shot away to the left but with sufficient spin to make it circle round and land on the fairway beyond the hazard.

My memory of the course as it was in my young days was of something much more demanding than what I came back to after a lapse of many years. The fairways were very restricted with bent grass and sand encroaching right to the edge. The only broad stretches of grass were the approach to Mount Zion (always my favourite) and possibly some holes over towards the Bowmore end (we rarely played the full course). Even the nature of the grass had changed from the permanently short springy Machrie turf to ordinary long grass (possibly the result of cattle having been grazed on the course in the interval, in my absence). This reminds me that, back in the twenties, as a schoolboy in the Ibrox/Bellahouston area of Glasgow I was told that the greens of the Bellahouston Bowling Club were being re-laid with turf specially imported from Machrie because of its close natural growth.

I also remember now that the Greenkeeper in my young days was Angus White who if I remember right was slightly lame in one leg but kept the greens in perfect order. I have not been down to Machrie for some years now, but I understand that the course has been restored to its former character.

In my day we did not play by 'numbers', we often used the same club for a variety of shots and distances. My favourite, an old Wm. Morris 'lofter', served for anything from a short chip from the edge of the green to a long iron-depending on how one played the shot. It could even lift the Maidens!'

Alastair's excellent memories are valuable in that they confirm stories from other sources even if not completely accurate in all details. The reference to Mr. Asquith having a set of McArthur etched clubs suggests the unique possibility of two Prime Ministers (A.J. Balfour was the other) having used etched golf clubs made on Islay. His reference to Ronald McArthur being 'the Artist' is perhaps wrong since his brother Sandy was a painter who was described in *Golf* of 1898 as 'The Artist'. The match between Taylor and Vardon was probably a practice round prior to the Islay Tournament in 1901, and finally the greenkeeper referred to would have been Willie White. For the conclusion to the story of Alastair Shanks refer to the Centenary Celebrations of Chapter 12.

There must be many other stories of golf on Islay which are worthy of being preserved for future generations. Hopefully, this chapter might be the catalyst which gets them written down and into the Islay Golf Club Archives.

CHAPTER TWELVE

CELEBRATING A CENTENARY

Islay Golf Club Celebrations

The principal events of the Centenary Celebrations took place over the weekend, Friday, 24th May 1991 to Sunday 26th. Most appropriately, it began on the Friday evening in the Machrie Hotel with a well attended Islay Malt Whisky tasting reception for members and principal guests. With introductions complete and 'thrapples' well lubricated, everyone moved to the Golfers Bar where Ailsa Smith, wife of Captain Billy Smith, unveiled the new trophy cabinet. The magnificent cabinet was constructed by master craftsman, Derick Renshaw, thanks to a generous gift from Alastair Shanks.

It had been planned that Mrs. Freda Ramsay would drive off the first official ball of the new century but due to ill-health she was unable to do so. She was represented by her daughter, Mrs. Joanna Ramsay Best and son Bruce who were both from Ontario, Canada. To Bruce fell the honour of driving the Islay Golf Club into its second century, at 10.30am on Saturday 25th May 1991. Using appropriately, an old Ronald McArthur iron, he stroked the ball confidently down the centre of the fairway, a fine achievement for a non-golfer.

Soon afterwards, the serious business began as John MacIntyre Jnr. hit the first shot for the Centenary Rosebowl, followed by some 63 golfers in this Stableford competition. In calm but misty conditions it was no great surprise when the course record holder, Iain Middleton won with 38 points.

More than 100 members gathered in the evening for the Centenary Dinner in the Machrie Hotel. The principal guests were Belle Robertson, M.B.E. and Sandy Sinclair O.B.E. D.L. It says much for the reputation of the Islay G.C. that they were able to call upon the services of these highly distinguished personalities from the world of amateur golf. Belle, who is arguably Scotland's most successful amateur lady golfer ever, played seven times in the Curtis Cup, had one win and

COMMITTEE OF MANAGEMENT
1990/1991

Captain
W. A. Smith

Vice-Captain
J. MacIntyre (Jnr.)

Immediate Past Captain
T. I. Irvine

J. Calder   D. MacKinnon
J. M. McGill   M. Heads
A. Brown   M. A. C. McNeill
J. McFarlane   J. Edgar
R. C. McGregor   A. Hyslop

CO-OPTED FOR CENTENARY
R. Middleton   R. Hardie
J. Campbell   A. McLachlan

CENTENARY COMMITTEE
W. A. Smith   D. MacKinnon
J. Calder   J. Mason
J. McGill   S. Grier
J. McFarlane   F. Grier
J. MacIntyre (Jnr.)   D. Brown

OFFICE BEARERS
Match Secretary   J. Callow
Secretary/Treasurer   T. Dunn

Committee of Management, 1990/91

Unveiling of New Trophy Cabinet. Speech by the Captain W. Smith.

Bruce Best prepares to drive off to start the 2nd Century of Islay G.C.
By Frazer McArthur

three seconds in the British Ladies Open Amateur Championship along with three successes in the British Ladies Stroke play Championship and seven appearances in the European Team Championship. On the home front she won the Scottish Ladies Amateur Championship seven times and was capped 16 times for Scotland in the Home Internationals.

Sandy couldn't quite match Belle's playing record. When he became Captain of the Royal and Ancient in 1989, he achieved the unique distinction of having won every single medal of the club. He was capped for Scotland in 1953, won one Glasgow and three Lanarkshire Championships and was twice Scottish Open Senior Amateur Champion. He excelled in the administration side of golf as well, having been President of the Scottish Golf Union, the European Amateur Golf Association and the Golf Foundation of Great Britain.

After a magnificent dinner, the Captain Bill Smith welcomed everyone and read out telegrams of congratulations from D.M. Marsh, Captain of the Royal & Ancient Golf Club, George McInnes from Edinburgh, and Gilbert Stevenson from Saudi Arabia. A special welcome was given to the far travelled Grant MacGregor from Australia. Belle Robertson, also a former Captain of Dunaverty G.C. in its Centenary year of 1989, very ably proposed the Centenary toast to the Islay Golf Club. The reply came from Past Captain John Calder, 'raconteur' of Laphroaig, who asked the members to muse on the differences which would prevail at the A.G.M. if the club owned the course. The absence of discussions on negotiations with the owners meant there would be nothing left to discuss!

The toast to the Game of Golf came from Sandy who told some stories about the Ayrshire golf legend, the late Hammy McInally. He arrived on the first tee one day, after a rum and coke breakfast, but forgot his golf shoes. Unperturbed, he played in his every day 'winkle -pickers' and broke the course record. Once after holing a long putt on the first green, his partner said, "Did ye no see that lump of dirt on the ball?" "Aye," said Hammy, "but a allowed fur it!"

It was 12.30am when Alastair MacLachlan replied with his usual brilliant witty speech. Among many other gems were: 'Roger Hardie is a keen golfer who doesn't work on Wednesdays because it interferes with two weekends and 'Lachie Mackinnon was once interrupted at the address by his caddie who told him he was addressing a mushroom'.

Belle presented the new Centenary Rose bowl to Ian Middleton and a replica Kildalton Cross was presented to Dianne Brown as winner of the Ladies Centenary Competition. A plaque was then presented to Belle by Sue Currie as a memento of the Centenary. After Bill Smith thanked everyone who helped to make the evening such a huge success, the historic evening (and morning) was concluded with a vote of thanks to the Chairman by Max McGill.

Etched club made by Ronald McArthur and used by Bruce Best.

Captain Bill Smith congratulates Bruce.

By Frazer McArthur

WELCOME	Captain W. A. Smith *Islay Golf Club*
GRACE	Mr. J. McFarlane, *Past Captain* *Islay Golf Club*
LOYAL TOAST	Mr. J. MacIntyre, *Vice Captain* *Islay Golf Club*
THE GUESTS	Captain W. A. Smith
	Mrs. Iain Ramsay Yr. of Kildalton *Grand-daughter-in-law of John Ramsay of Kildalton*
Toast to Islay Golf Club	Mrs. I. C. Robertson, M.B.E. *Dunaverty Golf Club*
Reply on behalf IGC	Mr. J. Calder, *Past Captain* *Islay Golf Club*
Toast to 'The Game of Golf'	Mr. A. Sinclair, O.B.E., D.L. *Past Captain, Royal and Ancient Golf Club of St. Andrews*
Reply to 'The Game of Golf'	Mr. A. McLachlan, M.A. (Hons.) *Islay Golf Club*
	Mr. J. Cubbage B.Sc., M.I.C.E. *Author/Historian of Islay Golf Club*

Turning back the clock – The Gowfers, l to rt., J. and O. Cubbage, A. MacLachlan, W. McRobb, P. and R. Hardie, E. Campbell, S. McMillan, M. Carmichael, S. McIntyre, M. Hedley, J. MacGregor, M. McGill, J. MacIntyre Snr., D. Brown, T. Dunn, R. MacGregor and R. Kidd.

By Frazer McArthur

Tom Dunn (alias Tom Morris)

A swirling mist was again present on Sunday morning to add a certain ethereal and authentic quality to the parade of some 18 stalwarts dressed in the fashion of golfers of 100 years ago. As they drove off the first tee using old wooden shafted clubs supplied by the author, the cameras and camcorders snapped furiously. The original intention was to play 3 holes but due to time limitations only one hole was possible before the start of the visitors v locals match - in normal attire! Murdo MacPherson fired his shotgun to start the match which finished all square at 6 1/2 matches each.

The final event of the weekend was a buffet dance organised by the Ladies. Some eighty members danced into the small hours to the music of Tosh and his Rhinns Ceilidh Band

Reflections on the Centenary weekend confirmed that the informal fun packed weekend had been a huge success. Not many golfers get the chance to participate in a golfing Centenary but for those privileged to join in the Islay Golf Club celebrations it was an experience never to be forgotten.

Regrettably, there was a sad side to the Centenary year with the death of the two principals who were responsible for the new trophy cabinet. Alastair Shanks, donor of the funds, died early in the year followed by Derick Renshaw just two months after its completion. Two Past Captains also passed away during the year, W.D. Calder and Forrest Anderson from Carluke.

Machrie Links and Hotel Centenary Celebrations

The blank Sunday of 14th July between the end of the Bells' Scottish Open and the start of the Open Championship was the day fixed by Murdo MacPherson for his contribution to the Centenary celebrations. It took the form of an Exhibition Match involving Alex Hay and Bruce Critchley of the B.B.C. television commentary team against professionals Brian Barnes and Bernard Gallacher. Due to having to play in the qualifying rounds of the Open the latter pair called off and were replaced by Mike Hughesden also of the B.B.C. team and Nigel Angus, a prominent Ayrshire golfer.

After a quick dash by car from the Scottish Open at Gleneagles to Glasgow Airport, a small plane chartered from Air Sinclair brought the team to Islay in time for the Machrie Centenary Dinner on the Saturday night. Guests included Islay G.C. members John MacIntyre Jnr., Tom Dunn and the author. A sumptuous dinner was presided over by Peter Halsall, President of the Machrie Golf Club. Peter, a member of Woburn G.C. was responsible for enticing his friends from the B.B.C. and Alex, professional at Woburn, to pay their first visit to Machrie.

Next morning a good crowd gathered for the 'Grand Match'. It was Scotland v England as Alex Hay, professional and director of the Woburn Golf Club, partnered

The Grand Match. Competitors and reception party, rt. to l., Tony McHale, Nigel Angus, Alex Hay, Murdo MacPherson, Peter Halsall, Bruce Critchley and Mike Hughesden (Bruce's two sons in front).

Alex Hay on First Tee.

Nigel Angus against the B.B.C. team of former Walker Cup player Bruce and his fellow Sunningdale G.C. member Mike. In glorious sunshine the B.B.C. team soon showed that they could make their clubs talk as well as they themselves did on T.V. An exciting ding dong battle ensued before the Scots arrived at the 18th tee one up. Any hopes the B.B.C. team had of salvaging a halved match disappeared as Alex holed a curly 12 yard putt on the last green to finish 2 up. At the presentation of prizes the four competitors were made Honorary Members of the Machrie G.C.(a short-lived Club run by the Hotel). Much praise was lavished on the course and its natural historic features. Sadly, Peter died in London early this year.

Centenary Inter-Club Matches

Three inter-club matches were also played at Machrie as part of the Centenary celebrations. It was a dual celebration for Lindrick G.C. and the Edinburgh City Chambers G.C. who were also celebrating their Centenary. Local rivals, Lochgilphead also paid a visit for a Centenary match. Players from all three clubs were full of praise for the course and the local hospitality. Of lesser importance were the results of the matches which were all won by the home team.

Where Eagles Dare

A unique flurry of 'eagles' at Machrie provided several Islay G.C. members with their own special memories of the Centenary year. A hint of what was to come arrived in 1990 when Thomas Logan holed in one at the 10th, the first ace reported for some years. Alex MacLean started the ball rolling in with his first ace at the 5th during Centenary week while playing in the Bowmore Plate and David Turner did likewise in practice for the Cross. Not to be outdone some of the older members got into the act also. While playing with his wife Mary, Ralph Middleton also got his eagle at the short 5th, followed in September by Past Captain John Campbell at the same hole. The last eagle of the season came two days later when another P.C., John MacIntyre Snr., saw his tee shot roll into the same hole. "I've been playing golf for over 40 years and there wasn't any person around to witness my first hole in one," said the delighted John. It was suggested that it was time to bring into use the new tee some 30 yards further back to make the hole a wee bit more difficult. Thanks are due to Tom Dunn for recording the above facts in Volume 1, Issue 1 of the new style Islay Links' newsletter in April 1992.

What a pleasant way to conclude a Centenary story as six golfers' dreams came true leaving countless others trying all that much harder to emulate their rare feat in the second century of the Islay Golf Club.

POSTSCRIPT

Newsflash 1

Just prior to going to print the news came through of the purchase of the Hotel and golf course by Malcolm King, a developer from England, who is making his first venture into the leisure industry. Prior to the meeting to discuss the future, and not least the fee for the coming year, a game of golf was arranged. Malcolm King was partnered by Tom Dunn against the Captain, Ralph Middleton, and Bob Hogben. Golf being golf with no quarters given, the latter were 1 up on the 5th tee when Malcolm, playing the course for the first time as owner, holed his 4 iron for his first ever hole in one! As he joins the select band above, one cannot help wondering, "Who writes the script?" Needless to say the next move was sharp right into the Machrie. The bar was closed but was soon opened and a very amiable and successful meeting was held which augurs well for the future success of the Islay Golf Club and the Machrie.

Newsflash 2

The Lagavulin Quaich has returned to Islay. Ninety-seven years after its legitimate departure from the Islay Golf Club, this magnificent trophy has been generously donated to the Golf Club by White Horse Distillers Ltd. Special thanks are due to Mr. R. Fresson, a director of White Horse Distillers Ltd., who realised the importance of the Quaich to the Islay Golf Club and arranged for its return to its original home.

APPENDICES

LIST OF CAPTAINS

1891-92	Major Lovat Ayshford Wise
1892-94	Hugh Morrison, Islay House
1894-96	P. J. Mackie, Lagavulin
1896-1906	J. S. Higginbotham
1906-07	Capt. Iain Ramsay of Kildalton
1907-09	John Buchanan
1909-11	P. D. Hendry
1911-12	P. Reid
1912-14	R. B. Mitchell
1914-20	Dr. D. P. M. Farquharson
1920-21	P. Reid
1921-22	J. G. Graham
1922-24	P. E. Soutter
1924-26	J. T. MacFarlane
1926-28	Dr. Murray
1928-29	John McBean
1929-30.	Dr. Chadborn
1930-32	Robert Paul
1932-33	M. Mactaggart
1933-34	A. D. Campbell
1934-35	J. Wilson
1935-36	Iain Mactaggart
1936-37	Dr. A. M. Campbell
1937-38	Wm. Walker, Foreland, Islay
1938-39	A. Wilson
1939-43	David Barbour
1943-44	-
1944-45	Wm. Walker, Foreland, Islay
1945-46	David Barbour
1946-47	Iain M. Mactaggart
1947-48	J. H. Keith
1948-49	J. R. H. Hall
1949-50	Dr. D. Riddell Campbell
1950-51	Dr. W. P. Soutter

1951-52	Ian Goodall
1952-53	W. White
1953-54	A. Gray
1954-55	R. C. MacGregor
1955-56	R. M. Wilson
1956-57	R. Grant
1957-58	T. Melville Lang
1958-59	H. Cairns
1959-60	W. Brownlee
1960-61	L. Mackinnon
1961-62	S. Hearder
1962-63	A. McNeill
1963-64	R. Gibb
1964-65	M. Ayres
1965-66	G. McInnes
1966-67	C. Guy
1967-68	D. Mackinnon
1968-69	J. B. Soutter
1969-70	F. Anderson
1970-71	J. MacIntyre
1971-72	M. McNeill
1972-73	J. W. Campbell
1973-74	A. Murdoch
1974-75	W. M. Sime
1975-76	J. Callow
1976-77	I. Wilson
1977-78	J. Mason
1978-79	J. Morrison
1979-80	S. Robertson
1980-81	D. F. Stone
1981-82	S. Grier
1982-83	J. MacFarlane
1983-84	W. D. Calder
1984-85	J. MacIntyre Snr
1985-86	R. C. MacGregor
1986-87	J. N. Calder
1987-88	M. McGill
1988-89	G. Stevenson

1989-90	T. Irvine
1990-91	W. A. Smith
1991-92	J. MacIntyre Jnr.
1992-93	M. A. C. McNeill
1993-94	M. Heads
1994-95	A. MacLachlan
1995-96	R. Middleton

WINNERS OF THE KILDALTON CHALLENGE CROSS
Presented by Mrs Ramsay of Kildalton in 1900

1900	Rev. J. E. Pease
1901	E. D. Evans
1902	W. A. Lambie, Glasgow
1903	L. McKay
1904	A. McVean
1905	J. E. Murray, Edinburgh
1906	P. Bolland, Islay
1907	J. S. Kennedy
1908	A. C. Hamilton
1909	C. A. McPherson
1910	P. D. Hendry
1911	D. W. Mitchell
1912	M. McIntyre
1913	S. P. Bolland
1914	J. S. Graham
1915-18	No competitions
1919	G. A. Cook
1920	P. E. Soutter
1921	J. S. Graham
1922	J. McBean
1923	D. M. Cameron
1924	J. S. Graham
1925	M. R. Armstrong
1926	S. W. Thompson
1927	J. S. Liddell
1928	R. M. Struthers
1929	R. M. Munro

1930	R. M. Munro
1931	R. M. Struthers
1932	P. E. Soutter
1933	R. C. MacGregor
1934	J. MacGregor
1935	R. C. MacGregor
1936	J. B. Soutter
1937	P. E. Soutter Jnr.
1938	J. A. Cruickshank
1939	P. E. Soutter Jnr.
1940-7	No competitions
1948	J. B. Soutter
1949	P. E. Soutter Jnr.
1950	R. C. MacGregor
1951	R. C. MacGregor
1952	A. Mackinnon
1953	A. Mackinnon
1954	D. McDougall
1955	I. Henderson
1956	D. MacCalman
1957	I. Henderson
1958	J. MacIntyre
1959	J. MacFarlane
1960	W. Brownlee
1961	I. McCuaig
1962	W. P. Soutter
1963	D. Mackinnon
1964	R. H. Gibb
1965	J. MacIntyre
1966	I. Mackinnon
1967	J. MacFarlane
1968	G. Stevenson
1969	L. Mackinnon
1970	A. D. MacKenzie
1971	J. L. Rintoul
1972	J. A. Mason
1973	W. I. Russell
1974	W. D. Calder

1975	W. M. P. Sime
1976	D. Gray
1977	D. Gray
1978	J. D. Gordon
1979	W. D. Calder
1980	D. Gray
1981	J. D. Gordon
1982	J. D. Gordon
1983	A. Livingstone
1984	A. MacFarlane
1985	J. Edgar
1986	J. MacIntyre Jnr.
1987	A. Holyoake
1988	G. R. Macgregor
1989	N. Macdonald
1990	J. F. Mason
1991	A. Holyoake
1992	S. Crawford
1993	I. Middleton
1994	D. Livingstone
1995	G. D. F. Macmillan

HIGGINBOTHAM TROPHY WINNERS

Trophy presented by Iain Ramsay Esq. of Kildalton in memory of J. S. Higginbotham, 1906

1906	J. S. Macdonald
1907	J. Bryce
1908	M. McIntyre
1909	R. S. Bollamd
1910	J. Bolland
1911	J. S. Macdonald
1912	R. S. Bolland
1913	M. McIntyre
1914	M. McIntyre
1915-18	No Competitions
1919-37	No results
1938	A. Mactaggart

Year	Winner
1939	D. Orr
1940-47	No Competitions
1948	No results
1949	W. White
1950	I. McCuaig
1951	W. White
1952	D. Mackinnon
1953	D. McInnes
1954-57	No results

Format now 2 ball foursomes

Year	Winner
1958	D. McDougall and A. Murdoch
1959	D. McDougall and I. McCuaig

Format now 18 hole stroke play

Year	Winner
1960	I. McCuaig
1961	J. MacIntyre
1962	A. MacKenzie
1963	A. MacKenzie
1964	A. Forsyth
1965	I. McCuaig
1966	J. Campbell
1967	J. Campbell
1968	R. Middleton
1969	W. Perrat
1970	R. Middleton
1971	W. Perrat
1972-74	No results
1975	J. Edgar
1976	J. Morrison
1977	I. McCuaig
1978	A. Thomson
1979	R. Baker
1980	D. Livingstone
1981	A. Brown
1982	I. McCuaig
1983	N. Mackinnon
1984	H. Jackson
1985	J. Edgar
1986	A. Livingstone

1987	J. Edgar
1988	J. Callow
1989	A. Holyoake
1990	R. MacIntyre
1991	J. MacIntyre Jnr.
1992	D. Holyoake
1993	R. MacIntyre
1994	K. Gillies
1995	K. McDonald

MACKIE QUAICH WINNERS
Presented by Peter J. Mackie, 1913

1914	Dr. Edgar Reid (Swansea)
1915-18	No competitions
1919	W. Patrick
1920	L. R. Hamilton
1921	P. E. Soutter
1922	A. C. Hamilton
1923-35	No results
1936	I. Kemp
1937	D. C. Orr (Hamilton)
1938	Jas. Leckie
after a tie with	J. H. Keith
1939	John Leckie
1940-47	No competitions
1948	W. Anderson
1949	A. Mackinnon
1950	D. Mackinnon
1951	D. McDougall
1952	W. White
1953	I. McCuaig
1954	W. Livingstone
1955	A. MacKenzie
1956	I. McCuaig
1957	A. MacKenzie
1958	A. MacKenzie
1959	J. MacFarlane
1960	A. MacKenzie

1961	J. MacFarlane
1962	C. Sweeney
1963	I. McCuaig
1964	A. MacKenzie
1965	A. Brown
1966	J. MacFarlane
1967	J. MacIntyre
1968	J. MacFarlane
1969	J. MacIntyre
1970	No result

WHITE HORSE TROPHY WINNERS

Presented by White Horse Distillers Ltd. to replace stolen Mackie Quaich

1971	J. Tannahill
1972-74	No results
1975	A. Cameron
1976	D. Heads
1977	J. MacIntyre Snr.
1978	J. MacIntyre Snr.
1979	J. MacIntyre Snr.
1980	J. MacIntyre Snr.
1981	J. MacIntyre Snr.
1982	A. Maclean
1983	I. McCuaig
1984	H. Jackson
1985	A. Livingstone
1986	A. Brown
1987	T. Logan
1988	J. Campbell
1989	R. Middleton
1990	R. MacIntyre
1991	D. Turner
1992	J. S. Edgar
1993	D. Holyoake
1994	R. Patterson
1995	A. Livingstone

CLUB CHAMPIONS

1964	I. McCuaig
1965	J. MacIntyre
1966	J. MacIntyre
1967	R. Gibb
1968	I. McCuaig
1969	I. McCuaig
1970	M. Gourlay
1971	R. Gibb
1972-74	No results
1975	J. Gordon
1976	L. Mackinnon
1977	D. S. Gray
1978	R. Hunter
1979	D. S. Gray
1980	G. Carnegie
1981	D.S. Gray
1982	J. Gordon
1983	I. Middleton
1984	R. Crighton
1985	A. Livingstone
1986	D. S. Gray
1987	J. S. Edgar
1988	D. S. Gray
1989	R. MacIntyre
1990	J. S. Edgar
1991	I. Middleton
1992	I. Middleton
1993	I. Middleton
1994	I. Middleton
1995	J. S. Edgar